I0213578

SIX LITTLE BUNKERS AT MAMMY JUNE'S

LAURA LEE HOPE

1st WORLD
LIBRARY
Literary Society

Six Little Bunkers at Mammy June's

Laura Lee Hope

© 1st World Library, 2006
PO Box 2211
Fairfield, IA 52556
www.1stworldlibrary.com
First Edition

LCCN: 2006907719

Softcover ISBN: 1-4218-2442-6
Hardcover ISBN: 1-4218-2342-X
eBook ISBN: 1-4218-2542-2

Purchase *"Six Little Bunkers at Mammy June's"*
as a traditional bound book at:
www.1stWorldLibrary.com/purchase.asp?ISBN=1-4218-2442-6

1st World Library is a literary, educational organization
dedicated to:

- Creating a free internet library of downloadable ebooks

  - Hosting writing competitions and offering book
    publishing scholarships.

Interested in more 1st World Library books?
contact: literacy@1stworldlibrary.com
Check us out at: www.1stworldlibrary.com

1st World Library Literary Society

Giving Back to the World

"If you want to work on the core problem, it's early school literacy."

- James Barksdale, former CEO of Netscape

"No skill is more crucial to the future of a child, or to a democratic and prosperous society, than literacy."

- Los Angeles Times

Literacy... means far more than learning how to read and write... The aim is to transmit... knowledge and promote social participation."

- UNESCO

"Literacy is not a luxury, it is a right and a responsibility. If our world is to meet the challenges of the twenty-first century we must harness the energy and creativity of all our citizens."

- President Bill Clinton

"Parents should be encouraged to read to their children, and teachers should be equipped with all available techniques for teaching literacy, so the varying needs and capacities of individual kids can be taken into account."

- Hugh Mackay

CONTENTS

CHAPTER I

AN ESKIMO IGLOO

"How could William get the croup that way?" Violet asked with much emphasis.

Of course, Vi was always asking questions - so many questions, indeed, that it was often impossible for her elders to answer them all; and certainly Rose and Russ Bunker, who were putting together a "cut-up" puzzle on the table, could not be bothered by Vi's insistence.

"I don't see how he could have got the croup that way," repeated the smaller girl. There were six of the little Bunkers, and Vi and Laddie were twins. She said to Laddie, who was looking on at the puzzle making: "Do you know how William did it, Laddie?"

Laddie, whose real name wasn't "Laddie" at all, but Fillmore Bunker, shook his head decidedly.

"I don't know," he told his twin sister. "Not unless it is a riddle: 'How did William get the croup?'"

"He hasn't got the croup," put in Rose, for just a moment giving the twins her attention.

"Why - ee!" cried Vi. "Aunt Jo said he had!"

"She didn't," returned Rose rather shortly and not at all politely.

"She did so!" rejoined Vi instantly, for although she and Rose loved each other very much they were not always in agreement. Vi's gray eyes snapped she was so vexed. "Aunt Jo said that a window got broke in - in the neu-ral-gi-a and William had to drive a long way yesterday and the wind blew on him and he got the croup."

"Was that the way of it?" said Laddie, thoughtfully. "Wait a minute, Vi. I've most got it -"

"You're not going to have the croup!" declared his twin. "You never had it! But I have had the croup, and I didn't catch it the way William did."

"No-o," admitted Laddie. "But - but I'm catching a new riddle if you'd only wait a minute for me to get it straight."

"Pooh!" said Vi. "Who cares anything about your old riddle? Br-r-r! it's cold in this room. Maybe we'll all get the croup if we can't have a better fire."

"It isn't the croup you mean, Vi," put in Rose again, but without stopping to explain to her smaller sister where and how she was wrong about William's illness.

"Say, Russ, why don't the steampipes hum any more?" broke in the voice of Margy, the next to the very littlest Bunker, who was playing with that latter very important person at one of the great windows overlooking the street.

Russ chuckled. He had just put the very last crooked piece of the puzzle into place.

"You don't expect to see humming birds in winter, do you, Margy?" he asked.

"Just the same, winter is the time for steampipes to hum," said Rose, shivering a little. "Oh! See! It's beginning to snow!"

Laura Lee Hope

"So 'tis," cried Russ, who was the oldest of the six. "Supposing it should be a blizzard, Rose Bunker?"

"S'posing it should!" repeated his sister, quite as much excited as Russ was at such a prospect.

"Buzzards fly and eat dead things. We saw 'em in Texas at Cowboy Jack's," announced Laddie, forgetting his riddle-making for the moment.

"That is right, Laddie," agreed Rose kindly. "But we're not talking about buzzards, but about blizzards. Blizzards are big snowstorms - bigger than you ever remember, I guess."

"Oh!" said Laddie doubtfully. "Were we talking about - about blizzards?"

"No, we weren't!" exclaimed Vi, almost stamping her foot. "We were talking about William's croup -"

"He hasn't got the croup, I tell you, Vi," Rose said wearily.

"He has. Aunt Jo -"

"In the first place," interrupted Rose quite decidedly, "only children have croup. It isn't a grown-up disease."

This announcement silenced even Violet for the moment. She stared at her older sister, round-eyed.

"Do - do diseases have to grow up, too?" she finally gasped.

"Oh, dear me, Vi Bunker!" exclaimed Rose, "I wish you didn't ask so many questions."

"Why not?" promptly inquired the smaller girl.

"We-ell, it's so hard to answer them," Rose frankly admitted. "Diseases don't grow up, I guess, but folks grow up and leave diseases like croup, and measles, and chicken-pox, behind them."

"And cut fingers and bumps?" asked Laddie, who had almost forgotten the riddle about William's croup that he was striving to make.

But Vi did not forget the croup. One could trust Vi never to forget anything about which she once set out to gather information.

"But how did William catch the croup through a broken window in the neu-ral-gi-a?" she demanded. "When I had croup I got my feet wet first."

"He hasn't got the croup!" Rose cried again, while Russ began to laugh heartily.

"Oh, Vi!" Russ said, "you got it twisted. William caught cold driving Aunt Jo's coupe with the window broken in it. He's got neuralgia from that."

"And isn't there any croup about it?" Laddie demanded rather sadly. "Then I'll have to start making my riddle all over again."

"Will that be awful hard to do, Laddie?" asked his twin. "Why! making riddles must be worse than having neu-ral-gi-a - or croup."

"Well, it's harder," sighed her brother. "It's easy to catch - Oh! Oh! Russ! Rose! I got it!"

"You haven't neuralgia, like poor William," announced Rose with confidence.

"Listen!" announced the glowing Laddie. "What is it that's so easy to catch but nobody runs after?"

"Huh! is that a riddle?" asked Russ.

"Course it's a riddle."

"A wubber ball," guessed Mun Bun, coming from the window against the panes of which the snow was now beating rapidly.

"No," Laddie said.

"A coupe!" exclaimed Violet.

"Huh! No!" said her twin in disdain.

Margy asked if he meant a kittie. She had been chasing one all over the house that morning while Russ and Rose had been to market with their aunt, and she did not think a kitten easy to catch at all.

"'Tisn't anything with a tail or claws," crowed the delighted Laddie.

"I bet it's that neuralgia William's got," laughed Russ.

"No-o. It isn't just that," his smaller brother said.

"And you'd better not say 'bet,' Russ Bunker," advised Rose wisely. "You know Aunt Jo says that's not nice."

"You just said it," Russ rejoined, grinning. "Twice."

"Oh, I never did!" cried his sister.

"Didn't you just say I'd 'better not say bet?'" demanded Russ. "Well, then count 'em! 'Bet' out of 'better' is one, and 'bet' makes two -"

"I never said it the way you did," began Rose, quite put out, when Laddie began to clamor:

"Tell me my riddle! You can't - none of you. 'What is it that's so easy to catch but nobody runs after?'"

"I don't know, Laddie," said Rose.

"I give it up," said Russ.

"Do you all give it up?" cried Laddie, almost dancing in his glee.

"What is it?" asked Vi.

"Why, the thing that's so easy to catch but nobody runs after, is a cold!" announced her twin very proudly.

"And I'm so-o cold," announced Mun Bun, hanging to Rose's skirt while the older ones laughed with Laddie. "Don't Aunt Jo ever have it warm in her house - like it is at home?"

"Of course she does, Mun Bun," said Rose, quickly hugging the little fellow. "But poor William is sick and nobody knows how to tend to the heating plant as well as he does. And so - Why, Russ, Mun Bun is cold! His hands are like ice."

"And so are my hands!" cried Margy, running hastily from the window. "We've been trying to catch the snowflakes through the windowpane."

"No wonder your hands are cold," said Rose admonishingly.

Russ began to cast about in his ingenious mind for some means of getting the younger children's attention off the discomfort of a room the temperature of which was down to sixty. In one corner were two stacks of sectional bookcases which Aunt Jo had just bought, but which had no books in them and no glass fronts. Russ considered them for a moment, and then looked all about the room.

"I tell you what," he said, slowly. "You know when they took us to the Sportsman's Show last week at Mechanic's Hall? Don't you remember about that Eskimo igloo that they had built of ice in the middle of the skating pond? Let's build an igloo like that, and get into it and keep warm."

"O-oo!" gasped Vi, "how can you do that?"

"Where will you get any ice?" Laddie demanded.

"Goodness! it's cold enough in here without bringing in ice," announced Rose with confidence.

"We won't build the igloo of ice blocks," said Russ quite calmly. "But we'll make believe it is ice."

"I'd rather do that," Laddie agreed. "For make-believe ice can't be so wet and cold as real ice, can it?"

"What you going to make your make-believe ice out of, Russ?" demanded Vi, the exceedingly practical.

Russ at once set them all to work, clearing the middle of the room and bringing up hassocks and small benches and some other articles that could be used in the construction of the indoor igloo. He brought the sections of the new bookcase, one piece at a time.

Russ really exhibited some skill in building up the walls of the hut in the middle of the floor. When it was completed it was rather a tight fit for all six of the little Bunkers to squeeze inside, but they did it. And the activities of building the igloo had warmed even Mun Bun.

"You know," said Rose thoughtfully, "Eskimos live in these igloos and eat blubber, and don't go out at all while it is snowing, same as it does now."

"Why don't they go out?" asked Vi.

"Because it is cold," said Russ.

"And why do they eat blubber?"

"Because they are hungry," said Rose.

"What's blubber, anyway?" asked the inquisitive one. "Is it like candy?"

"It's more like candles," answered Russ, laughing.

Just then Laddie kicked excitedly.

"I bet I can make another riddle!" he cried.

"Now, you see, Russ Bunker?" Rose admonished. "Laddie has got that word, too."

"Hey, stop kicking, Laddie!" cried Russ.

But in his excitement the boy twin had put his foot right through the wall of the igloo! At least, he had kicked one of the boxes out of place and the whole structure began to wobble.

"Oh! Oh! Oh!" shrieked Vi. "It's falling."

"Get Mun Bun out," gasped Rose, thinking first of all of the littlest Bunker.

But just then the heaped up boxes came down with a crash and the six little Bunkers were buried under the ruins of their "igloo."

Laura Lee Hope

CHAPTER II

THE SNOWMAN

A corner of one of the overturned bookcase sections struck Russ Bunker's head with considerable force - actually cutting the skin and bringing blood. Big as he was, the oldest Bunker yelled loudly.

Then, of course, everybody yelled. Quite a panic followed. When Aunt Jo and Mother Bunker came running to the front room where all this had taken place the Eskimo igloo looked very much like a pile of boxes with a young earthquake at work beneath it!

"For the good land's sake!" gasped Aunt Jo, who usually was very particular about her speech, but who on this occasion was startled into an exclamation. "What is happening?"

"Get off my head, Vi!" wailed Laddie, from somewhere under the tottering pile. "It's not to sit on."

"Oh! Oh!" cried Rose. "Russ is all bloody! Oh, dear!"

"I'm not cold any more," cried Mun Bun. "Let me out! I'll be good!"

But Russ Bunker was neither crying nor struggling. He was a good deal of a man, for a nine-and-a-half-year-old boy. Being the oldest of the six little Bunkers there were certain duties which fell to his lot, and he understood that one of them was to keep cool when anything happened to excite or frighten his brothers and sisters.

The whack he had got on the head, and even the trickle of blood down his face, did not cause Russ to lose his head. No, indeed. He, and the other little Bunkers, had been in innumerable scrapes before, and the wreck of the Eskimo igloo was nothing provided Aunt Jo did not make a lot out of it. It just crossed Russ' mind that he ought to have asked his aunt before he used the sectional bookcases for building-blocks.

Naturally of an inventive turn of mind, Russ was constantly building new things - make-believe houses, engines, automobiles, steamboats, and the like - usually with a merry whistle on his lips, too. He was a cheerful boy and almost always considered the safety and pleasure of his brothers and sisters first.

In companionship with Rose, who was a year younger, the boy cared for the other four little Bunkers so successfully that Mother Bunker and Daddy Bunker were seldom troubled in their minds regarding any of the children. Rose was a particularly helpful little girl, and assisted Mother Bunker a good deal. She was a real little housewife.

Vi and Laddie, the twins, were both very active children - active with their tongues as well as their bodies. Violet's inquisitiveness knew no bounds. She wanted to know about every little thing that happened about her. Daddy Bunker said he was sure she must ask questions in her sleep. Laddie was an inveterate riddle-asker. He learned every riddle he heard; and he tried to make up riddles about everything that happened. Sometimes he was successful, and sometimes he was not. But he always tried again, having a persevering temperament.

The smallest Bunkers - Margy, whose real name was Margaret, and Mun Bun, whose real name was Monroe Ford - were quite as anxious to get out from under the heap of boxes as the others. Mother Bunker and Aunt Jo ran to their assistance, and soon the six were on their feet to be hugged and scolded a little by both their mother and aunt.

"But they do get into such mischief all the time," sighed Mother Bunker. "I shall be glad when Daddy gets back and decides what to do for the winter. I don't know whether we shall go right back to Pineville or not."

For it was in Pineville, Pennsylvania, that we first met the six little Bunkers and in the first volume of this series went with them on a nice vacation to Mother Bunker's mother. The book telling of this is called "Six Little Bunkers at Grandma Bell's."

After that lovely visit in Maine the six little Bunkers had gone to stay for a time with each of the following very delightful relatives and friends: To Aunt Jo's in Boston, where they were now for a second visit over the Thanksgiving holidays; to Cousin Tom's; to Grandpa Ford's; to Uncle Fred's; to Captain Ben's; and last of all to Cowboy Jack's.

In that last book, "Six Little Bunkers at Cowboy Jack's," they had enjoyed themselves so much that they were always talking about it. And now, as Vi managed to crawl out from under the wreck of the Eskimo igloo, she announced:

"That iggilyoo isn't half as nice to live in as Chief Black Bear's wigwam was at Cowboy Jack's. You 'member that wigwam, Russ?"

"I remember it, all right," said Russ, rather ruefully touching the cut above his temple and bringing away his finger again to look at the blood upon it. "Say, is it going to keep right on bleeding, Mother?"

"Not for long," declared Mother Bunker. "But I think you were rightly punished, Russ. Suppose the corner of the section had cut Mun Bun's head?"

"I should have been awful sorry," admitted Russ. "I guess I didn't think much, Mother. I was only trying to amuse 'em 'cause they were cold."

"It is cold in here, Amy. Don't scold the boy. See! The storm is getting worse. I don't know what we shall do about the fire. Parker and Annie don't seem to know what to do about the heater and I'm sure I don't. Oh, dear!"

"B-r-rrr!" shivered Mother Bunker. "I am not fond of your New England winters, Jo. I hope we shall go South -"

"Oh, Mother!" cried Rose excitedly. "Shall we really go down South with Daddy? Won't that be glorious?"

"I guess it's warm down there," said Laddie. "Or maybe the steampipes hum."

"Do the steampipes hum down South?" asked Violet.

While the four older children were exceedingly interested in this new proposal for excitement and adventure, Margy and Mun Bun had returned to the great window that overlooked the street and the front steps. They flattened their noses against the cold pane and stared down into the driving snow. Within this short time, since the storm had begun, everything was white and the few people passing in the street were like snowmen, for the white flakes stuck to their coats and other wraps.

"Oh, see that man!" Margy cried to Mun Bun. "He almost fell down."

"He's not a man," said her little brother with confidence. "He's a boy."

"Oh! He's a black boy - a colored boy. That's right, so he is."

The figure in the snow stumbled along the sidewalk, clinging to the iron railings. When he reached the steps of Aunt Jo's house he slipped down upon the second step and seemed unable to get up again. His body sagged against the iron railing post, and soon the snow began to heap on him and about him.

"Oh!" gasped Margy. "He is a reg'lar snowman."

"He's a black snowman," said Mun Bun. "It must be freezing cold out there, Margy."

"Of course it is. He'll turn into a nicicle if he stays there on the steps," declared the little girl, with some anxiety.

"And he hasn't a coat and scarf like you and me," Mun Bun said. "Maybe he hasn't any Grandma Bell to knit scarfs for him."

"I believe we ought to help him, Mun Bun," said Margy, decidedly. "We have plenty of coats."

"And scarfs," agreed Mun Bun. "Let's."

So they immediately left the room quite unnoticed by the older people in it. This is a remarkable fact. Whenever Margy and Mun Bun had mischief in mind they never asked Mother about it. Now, why was that, do you suppose?

The two little ones went swiftly downstairs into the front hall. Both had coats and caps and scarfs hung on pegs in a little dressing-room near the big door. They knew that they should not touch the outer garments belonging to the older children; but they got their own wraps.

"Maybe he's too big for them," murmured Margy. "But I guess he can squeeze into the coats - into one of them, anyway."

"Course he can," said Mun Bun. "Mine's a nawful warm coat. And that black snowman isn't much bigger than I am, Margy."

"I don't know," said his sister slowly, for she was a little wiser than Mun Bun about most things. "Open the door."

Mun Bun could do that. This was the inside door, and they stepped into the vestibule. Pressing his face close to the glass of one of the outer doors, Mun Bun stared down at the "black snowman" on the step.

"He's going to sleep in the snow," said the little boy. "I guess we've got to wake him up, Margy."

He pounded on the glass with his fat fist. He knocked several times before the figure below even moved. Then the colored boy, who was not more than seventeen or eighteen, turned his head and looked up over his shoulder at the faces of the two children in the vestibule.

He was covered with snow. His face, though moderately black as a usual thing, was now gray with the cold. His black eyes, even, seemed faded. He was scantily clad, and his whole body was trembling with the cold.

"Come up here!" cried Mun Bun, beckoning to the strange boy. "Come up here!"

The boy in the snow seemed scarcely to understand. Or else he was so cold and exhausted that he could not immediately get up from the step on which he was sitting.

Laura Lee Hope

CHAPTER III

UNCLE SAM'S NEPHEW

The fluffy, sticky snowflakes gathered very fast upon the colored boy's clothing. As Mun Bun had first announced, he looked like a snowman, only his face was grayish-black.

He was slim, and when he finally stood up at the bottom of the house steps, he seemed to waver just like a slim reed in the fierce wind that drove the snowflakes against him. He hesitated, too. It seemed that he scarcely knew whether it was best to mount the steps to Aunt Jo's front door or not.

"Come up here!" cried Mun Bun again, and continued to beckon to him through the glass of the outer door.

Margy held up her coat and cap, and beckoned to the boy also. He looked much puzzled as he slowly climbed the steps. His lips moved and the children knew he asked:

"What yo' want of me, child'en?"

Mun Bun tugged at the outer door eagerly, and finally it flew open. He shouted in the face of the driving snow:

"Come in here, snowman. Come in here!"

"I ain't no snowman," drawled the colored boy. "But I sure is as cold as a snowman could possibly be."

"It's warmer inside here than it is out there," Margy said. "Although we're not any too warm. Our steampipes don't hum. But you come in."

"Yes," said Mun Bun, grabbing at the colored boy's cold, wet hand. "You come in here. We have some coats and things you can put on so you won't be cold."

"Ma goodness!" murmured the boy, staring at the garments the children held out to him.

"You can wear 'em," said Margy. "We have more."

"You put on my coat," urged Mun Bun. "It's a boy's coat. You won't want Margy's, for she's a girl."

"Ma goodness!" ejaculated the colored boy again, "what yo' child'en s'pose I do wid dem t'ings? 'Less I puts 'em up de spout?"

The two children hadn't the first idea as to what he meant by putting the clothing up the spout. But the colored boy meant that he might pawn them and get some money. He did not offer to take the coats and other things that Margy and Mun Bun tried to put into his hands.

Just at this moment Mother Bunker and Aunt Jo, followed by Russ and Rose, appeared on the stairs. They had missed the two little folks and, as Aunt Jo had said, wrinkling her very pretty nose, that she could "just smell mischief," they had all come downstairs to see what the matter was.

The colored boy spied them. He had evidently been ill used by somebody, for he was very much frightened. He thrust the coats back at the children and turned to get out of the vestibule.

But the door had been sucked to by the wind and it was hard to open again. It was really quite wonderful that Mun Bun had been able to get it open when he and Margy had called the strange colored boy in.

"Don't go!" cried Margy.

"Take my coat, please," urged Mun Bun. "I know it will keep you warm."

And all the time the colored boy was tugging at the handle of the outer door and fairly panting, he was so anxious to get out. Mother Bunker was the first to reach the door into the vestibule, and she opened it instantly.

"Wait!" she commanded the strange boy. "What do you want? What are you doing here?"

But by this time the young fellow had jerked open the outer door, and now he darted out and almost dived down the snowy steps.

"Oh, Mother!" cried Mun Bun, "he's forgot his coat and cap and scarf. I wanted him to wear mine because he was so cold and snowed on."

"And he could have had mine, too," declared Margy quite as earnestly.

"What do these tots mean?" gasped Aunt Jo, holding up both hands.

But Mother Bunker, who understood her little Bunkers very well indeed, in a flash knew all about it. She cried:

"The poor boy! Bring him back! He did look cold and wet."

"Oh, he's just a tramp," objected Aunt Jo.

"He's poor, Josephine, and unfortunate," answered Mother Bunker, as though that settled all question as to what they should do about the colored boy.

Russ Bunker had already got his cap and mackinaw. He darted out of the house, down the steps, and followed the shuffling figure of the colored boy, now all but hidden by the fast-driving snow. How it did snow, to be sure!

"Say! Wait a minute!" Russ called, and caught the strange youth by the elbow.

"What yo' want, little boy?" demanded the other. "I ain't done nothin' to them child'en. No, I ain't. Dey called me up to dat do' or I wouldn't have been there."

"I know that," said Russ, urgently detaining him. "But come back. My mother wants to speak to you, and I guess my Aunt Jo'll treat you nice, too. You're cold and hungry, aren't you?"

"Sure is," groaned the boy.

"Then they will give you something to eat and let you get warm. You'd better come," added Russ very sensibly, "for it looks as if it would be a big storm."

"Sure do," agreed the colored boy again. "Ah don' like dis snow. Don't have nothin' like dis down whar I come fom. No, suh."

"Now, come on," said Russ eagerly. "My mother's waiting for us."

The negro lad hesitated no longer. Even Russ saw how weary and weak he was as he stumbled on beside him. His shoes were broken, his trousers were very ragged, and his coat that he had buttoned up closely was threadbare. His cap was just the wreck of a cap!

"Yo' sure she ain't goin' to send for no policeman, little boy?" queried the stranger. "I wasn't goin' to take them clo'es.

No, suh!"

"She understands," said Russ confidently, and holding to the boy's ragged sleeve led him up the steps of Aunt Jo's pretty house.

Russ saw Mr. North, the nice old gentleman who lived over the way, staring out of his window at this surprising fact: Aunt Jo allowing a beggar to enter at her front door! Still, Mr. North, as well as the rest of the neighbors, had decided before this that almost anything astonishing could happen while the six little Bunkers were visiting their Aunt Jo in Boston's Back Bay district.

"Here he is, Mother," said Russ, entering the hall with the colored boy.

The other children had come downstairs now and all understood just what Margy and Mun Bun had tried to do for the stranger. Mother Bunker smiled kindly upon the wretched lad, even if Aunt Jo did look on a little doubtfully from the background.

"We understand all about it, boy," Mother Bunker said. "The little folks only wanted to help you; and so do we. Do you live in Boston?"

"Me, Ma'am? No, Ma'am! I lives a long way souf of dis place. Dat I do!"

"And have you no friends here?"

"Friends? Whar'd I get friends?" he demanded, complainingly. "Dey ain't no friends for boys like me up Norf yere."

"Oh! What a story!" exclaimed Aunt Jo. "I know people must be just as kind in Boston as they are in the South."

"Mebbe dey is, lady," said the colored boy, looking somewhat frightened because of Aunt Jo's vigorous speech. "Mebbe dey is; but dey hides it better yere. If yo' beg a mess of vittles in dis town dey puts yo' in jail. Down Souf dey axes you is you hongry? Ya-as'm!"

At that Aunt Jo began to bustle about to the great delight of the children. She called down to Parker, the cook, and asked her to put out a nice meal on the end of the kitchen table and to make coffee. And then she said she would go up to the attic where, in a press in which she kept garments belonging to a church society, there were some warm clothes that might fit the colored boy.

Rose and Vi went with Aunt Jo to help, or to look on; but Margy and the three boys stayed with their mother to hear more that the visitor might say.

"My name's Sam," he replied to Mother Bunker's question. "Dat is, it's the name I goes by, for my hones'-to-goodness name is right silly. But I had an Uncle Sam, and I considers I has got a right to be named after him. So I is."

"Does your Uncle Sam wear a tall hat and red-and-white striped pants with straps under the bootsoles and stars on his vest?" asked Laddie, with great interest and eagerness.

"I dunno, little fellow," said Sam. "I ain't never seen my Uncle Sam, but I heard my mammy talk about him."

Russ and his mother were much amused at Laddie's question. Russ said:

"That Uncle Sam you are talking about, Laddie, is a white man. He couldn't be this Sam's uncle."

"Why not?" demanded Laddie, with quite as much curiosity as his twin sister might have shown.

"Very true, why not?" repeated Mrs. Bunker, with some

gravity. "You are wrong, Russ. Our Uncle Sam is just as much this Sam's uncle as he is ours. Now go down to the kitchen, Sam. I hear Parker calling for you. Eat your fill. And wait down there, for we shall want to see you again."

CHAPTER IV

DADDY'S NEWS

Aunt Jo found the garments she meant to give to Sam, the strange colored boy, and she and Rose and Vi came downstairs with them to the room in which the children had been playing at first. Russ and Laddie had set up the sectional bookcase once more and the room looked less like the wreck of an auction room, Mother Bunker said.

She had returned with Margie and the boys. They thought it better - at least, the adults did - to leave Sam in the kitchen with Parker and Annie, the maid.

"But I hate to see that boy go away from here in this storm," said kind-hearted Aunt Jo. "Perhaps what he says about us Boston people in comparison with those where he comes from, is true. The police do arrest people for begging."

"Well, we have tramps at Pineville," Mother Bunker observed. "But the constable doesn't often arrest any. Not if they behave themselves. But a city is different. And this boy did not know how to ask for help, of course. Don't you think you can be of help to him, Jo?"

"I'll see," said Aunt Jo. "Wait until he has had a chance to eat what Parker has fixed for him."

Just then Annie, the parlormaid, tapped on the door.

"Please'm," she said to Aunt Jo, "that colored boy is goin' down in the cellar to fix the furnace."

"To fix the furnace?" cried Aunt Jo.

"Yes'm. He says he has taken care of a furnace before. He's been up North here for 'most two years. But he lost his job last month and couldn't find another."

"The poor boy," murmured Mother Bunker.

"Yes'm," said Annie. "And when he heard that the house was cold because me nor Parker didn't know what to do about the furnace, and the fire was most out, he said he'd fix it. So he's down there now with Parker and Alexis."

"Did Alexis come home?" cried Russ, who was very fond, as were all the Bunker children, of Aunt Jo's great Dane. "Can't we go down and see Alexis?"

"And see Sam again," said Margy. "Me and Mun Bun found him, you know."

It seemed to the little girl as though the colored boy had been quite taken away from her and from Mun Bun. They had what Mother Bunker laughingly called "prior rights" in Sam.

"Well, if he is a handy boy like that," said Aunt Jo, referring to the colored boy, "and can fix the furnace, we shall just have to keep him until William is well again. Has he finished his dinner, Annie?"

"Not yet, Ma'am. And indeed he was hungry. He ate like a wolf. But when he heard about us all being beat by that furnace, down he went. There! He's shaking the grate now. You can hear him. He said the ashes had to be taken out from under the grate or the fire never would burn. Yes'm."

"Well, then," said Mother Bunker, "you children will have to wait to see Sam - and Alexis - until he has finished eating."

"Annie," said Aunt Jo quickly, before the girl could go, "how does Alexis act toward this boy?"

"Oh, Ma'am! Alexis just snuffed of him, and then put his head in his lap. Alexis says he's all right. And for a black person," added the parlormaid, "I do think the boy's all right, Ma'am."

She went out and Aunt Jo and Mother Bunker laughed. The youngsters were suddenly excited at that moment by the stopping of a taxicab at the door. Vi had spied it from the window, for hard as it snowed she could see that.

"Here's Daddy! Here's Daddy!" she cried, dancing up and down.

Mun Bun and Margy joined in the dance, while the other three children entered upon a whirlwind rush down the stairway to meet Mr. Bunker at the front entrance.

He came in, covered with snow, and with his traveling bag. The children's charge upon him would surely have overturned anybody but Daddy Bunker.

"I scarcely dare come home at all," he shouted up the stairway to his wife and Aunt Jo, "because of these young Indians. You would think they were after my very life, if you didn't know that it was my pockets they want to search."

He shook off the clinging snow and the clinging children until he had removed his overcoat. Russ grabbed up the bag, and Rose and Laddie each captured an arm and were fairly carried upstairs by Mr. Bunker. He landed breathless and laughing with them in the middle of the big room which Aunt Jo had given up to the six little Bunkers as their playroom while they visited here in her Back Bay home.

"What is the news, Charles?" asked Mother Bunker, almost as

eagerly as the children themselves might have asked the question.

"I've got to see Armatage personally - that is all there is about it, and Frank Armatage cannot come North."

"Then you are going?" said his wife, and the children almost held their several breaths to catch Daddy Bunker's reply.

Their father looked around upon the eager little faces. Then he glanced at his wife and smiled.

"What do you think?" he asked. "Had I better say before so many little pop-eyed, curious folk? I - don't - know -"

"Oh, Daddy!" gasped Rose.

"We want to go with you," breathed Russ.

"I want to go!" cried Vi. "Where is it?"

"If Vi goes, can't I go too?" Margy pleaded.

"I'm not going to stay here, Daddy, if the rest go," declared Laddie.

But Mun Bun just walked gravely over to his father and put up both his arms.

"Mun Bun go with Daddy," he said confidently.

"The blessed baby!" cried Aunt Jo.

"It doesn't look much as though they appreciated your hospitality, Josephine," said Daddy Bunker to his sister, smiling over the top of Mun Bun's head as he held the little fellow.

"Oh!" cried Rose instantly, "we have had an awfully nice time here. We always do have nice times here. But we want to go with Daddy, and so does Mother."

"Two words for yourself and one for me, Rose," laughed her mother. "But if it is going to take some time, Charles, I think we would all like to go along."

"I had Mr. Armatage on the long distance telephone," said Daddy Bunker, smiling. "He was in Savannah. His plantation is some distance from that city. And he has invited us all to spend the Christmas holidays with him at his country home. What do you think of that?"

It was pretty hard for Mother Bunker to say what she thought of it because of the gleeful shouts of the children. It did not much matter to Russ, and Rose, and Violet, and Laddie, and Margy, and Mun Bun where they went with Daddy Bunker. It was just the idea of going to some new place and to have new adventures.

"Well," said the gentleman finally, "the boat sails day after to-morrow. Believing that you would approve, Amy, and knowing Jo couldn't go, I have already secured reservations for us eight Bunkers - two big staterooms. The boat is the *Kammerboy*, of the Blue Pennant Line."

The six little Bunkers were so delighted by this news and the prospect of a boat journey into warmer waters than those that ebb and flow about Boston, that they almost forgot the colored boy whose entry into the house had been brought about by Margy and Mun Bun.

But the latter, sitting in Daddy's lap, a little later began to prattle about his "black snowman," and so the story of Sam came out.

By that time the steampipes were humming and the whole house was warm and cozy again.

"And we can thank Sam for that, Charles," said Mother Bunker. "William is ill, and you would have had to go down and fight that furnace if this boy had not come along and proved himself so handy."

"Maybe we'd all better go down and thank him," said Rose soberly.

Daddy Bunker laughed. "I guess you want to get better acquainted with this wonderful Sam," he said. "A right nice boy, is he, Mother Bunker?"

"He seems to be," agreed Mother Bunker. "And he certainly needed friends. I think Jo will keep him for a while. At least, as long as William is laid up."

A little later the children all trooped down to the big kitchen. The good-natured cook did not mind their presence. And Alexis, the great Dane, showed plainly that he was delighted to see his young playfellows. Alexis was a very intelligent dog and it was no wonder that the servants and Aunt Jo considered that anybody of whom the dog approved must be "all right." Alexis had approved of Sam.

Sam had recovered from his weariness, and, no longer hungry and his next few meals in prospect, his spirits had rebounded from their low ebb to cheerfulness. The kindness shown him, and the praise the women had heaped upon him because of his mastery of the difficult furnace, delighted Sam.

"I'm sure obliged to you child'en for as'in' me into this yere house," he said, grinning at Margy and Mun Bun. "Dis is sure just as fine folks as we have down Souf. Dey done fed de hongry an' clothed de naked. An' mighty good clo'es, too."

He had on the suit Aunt Jo had found for him and almost new shoes, while an overcoat and a hat which he was to wear when he went out hung behind the cellar door. There was a small room off the kitchen in which Sam was to sleep. To the colored boy's mind he was "right good fixed."

"Let me have dat mouf organ, little boy," said Sam, observing Laddie's harmonica. "I show yo' sumpin'. Now, cl'ar de way. I's goin' to work de mouf organ and dance fo' yo'."

The women stopped in their work to watch him, as well as the children. Sam slid out into the middle of the floor, began to jerk a tune out of the harmonica, and commenced a slow dance - a sort of double shuffle.

But he soon pivoted and slid much faster, all in time with the sounds he drew from the harmonica. Annie and Parker applauded his unexpected steps, and the children began to shriek in delight.

"Now we has it!" exclaimed Sam, removing the instrument from between his lips, and panting from his exertions. "Now we skates down de floor. Now, turn again and back-along. I's a-comin', child'en - I's a-comin'. See me dance Jim Crow! Here I comes and dere I goes! Now, de pigeon-wing -"

He cut a most surprising figure, both hands flapping in the air and his slim body bent and twisted at a curious angle. With a resounding slap of the sole of his shoe on the floor he brought the dance to an end and fell panting into his chair.

"You're some dancer, Sam," cried the eager Annie. "Ain't he, Parker?"

"What do you call that figure?" demanded Parker. "A pigeon-wing?"

"Dat's what it is," breathed Sam, smiling widely. "My own particular invention, dat is. Nobody can't do dat like I can. No, suh!"

Just then their Mother called the six little Bunkers upstairs, and they had to leave the kitchen. But they would all have liked to see Sam cut that pigeon-wing again.

CHAPTER V

OFF FOR SUMMER SEAS

How busy the six little Bunkers were on the next day you can easily imagine. Such a packing of bags and steamer trunks! Though of course Mother Bunker did most of that, although Rose helped some. And such a running about the bedrooms and upper halls of Aunt Jo's house asking if this thing shouldn't be put in, or that thing shouldn't be left out!

The little people could think of more articles that might be needed down South than ten grown-ups could imagine! Laddie was sure they would need their bathing suits that they had had at Captain Ben's. Mun Bun, who had been playing with Margy in the yard making big snowballs, came in to ask his mother if they couldn't take just one of the biggest snowballs with them in one of the trunks, because Sam, the colored boy, said there wouldn't be any snow down South.

"But, my dear!" exclaimed Mother Bunker, laughing, "we are going down South just to escape the snow and the cold. Why carry it with us?"

"But maybe the little boys and girls down there will want to see some real snow," said Mun Bun, who could almost always find an answer for any question like this.

"Then they will have to come up North to see it," declared his mother decidedly. "We cannot take snow along on the boat, that is sure."

Violet found at least a hundred brand new questions to ask
about the preparations for the trip. Mother Bunker finally
called her a "chatterbox" and begged her to stop.

"How do you suppose I can attend to a dozen different things
at once, Violet, and answer your questions, too?"

"Never mind the things, Mother," Vi replied. "Just tell me -"

"Not another question!" exclaimed Mother Bunker. "Stop it!"

And then she put out her hand for something to put in the
trunk she was packing, and actually squealed when her hand
unexpectedly met Alexis's cold, damp nose.

"Goodness me!" cried Mother Bunker. "That dog is a
nuisance. That is the third time, at least, that I have tried to
pack his nose in this trunk. Every time I reach out for
something he thinks I want to pet him."

This delighted Margy and Mun Bun very much. The idea of
packing the great Dane in a steamer trunk was really quite
ridiculous. Violet did not venture any more questions immediately however; but Laddie suddenly broke out with a new
riddle.

"Oh, Mother! Mother!" he cried. "Do you know the difference
between a dog and an elephant?"

"I should hope so!" Mother Bunker said, chuckling. "But I
suppose you want me to give the riddle up so that you can
have the pleasure of telling me what the difference is between
Alexis and an elephant."

"Not just Alexis; any dog," urged Laddie. "And, of course, it
would be real polite of you if you said you didn't know,"
added the little boy.

"Very well; what is the difference between an elephant and a dog, Laddie?"

"Why," cried Laddie very eagerly, "an elephant owns a trunk of his very own; and a dog only wants to get into a trunk. There now!"

"But all dogs don't want to get into trunks," objected Vi. "Do they? Do they, now, Mother?"

"I am afraid Laddie's riddle is not as good as some he makes up," said Mother Bunker. "For you know, dogs have trunks as well as elephants."

Her eyes twinkled as she said it, for she knew she was going to puzzle her little brood. At once they all broke out with questions and exclamations. How could that be? They had seen, as Vi said, "oceans of dogs" and none of them had had a nose long enough to be called a trunk, like the elephants they had seen at the circus.

"Mother is just puzzling us," Laddie said. "How can a dog have a trunk when his nose is short and blunt? At least, most dogs' noses are short and blunt."

"Each dog has a trunk nevertheless," declared Mother Bunker, laughing. "And so have you, and so have I."

"I have a suitcase," announced Mun Bun gravely. "I don't have a trunk."

Mother Bunker swept Mun Bun into her arms then and kissed his chubby neck.

"Of course you have a trunk, honey-boy," she cried. "All your little body between your shoulders and your legs is your trunk. So you all have trunks, and so do the dogs."

The children laughed delightedly at this, but Laddie suddenly stopped laughing.

"Why!" he cried out in great glee, "then the elephant, Mother, has two trunks. I guess I can make a *good* riddle out of that, can't I?"

Russ and Rose took Alexis downstairs after that so that he would not be in the way. They wanted to see Sam again, anyway. And they asked him to dance for them.

"I'm going to learn how to cut that pigeon wing," Russ declared. "You do it again, please, Sam. I ought to be able to learn it if I see you do it often enough."

However, Russ did not succeed in this ambition. There really was not time for him to learn the trick, for the next morning, very early, the Bunker family started for the boat. The snowstorm had long since ceased, and the streets had been cleaned. William had recovered from his attack of neuralgia and drove them in the big closed car to the dock where the *Kammerboy* lay.

It was a great white steamer with three smoke stacks and a wireless mast. There was so much to see when they first went aboard that the six little Bunkers could not possibly observe everything with only two eyes apiece! They wanted to be down in the saloon and in the staterooms that Daddy Bunker had engaged and out on the deck all at the same time. And how were they to do that?

Russ and Rose, however, were allowed to go out on deck and watch the ship get out of the dock and steam down the harbor. But Mother Bunker at first kept the four smaller children close to her side.

"I never knew Boston was so big," said Rose, as they looked back at the smoky city. "I guess Aunt Jo never showed us all of it, did she, Russ?"

"I don't suppose if we lived there a whole year we should be able to see it all," declared her brother wisely. "Maybe we could see it better from an airplane. I'd like to go up in an airplane."

"No, no! Don't do that, Russ! Maybe the engine would get stalled like the motor-car engine does, and then you couldn't get down," said Rose, very much worried by this thought.

"Well, we could see the city better."

"We can see it pretty well from here," said Rose. "And see the islands. There is a lighthouse, Russ. Would you like to live in a lighthouse?"

"Yes, I would, for a while," agreed her brother. "But I'd rather be right on this boat, sailing out into the ocean. Just think, Rose! We've never been away out at sea before."

"There was lots of ocean at Captain Ben's," said the girl. "I suppose the ocean is all the same everywhere. Just water. I hope it stays flat."

"Stays flat?" repeated Russ, opening his eyes very wide.

"Yes," said Rose gravely. "I don't like water when it's bumpy. It makes me feel funny in my stomach when it's that way."

"Oh! It won't be rough," said Russ, with much assurance. "I heard Daddy say we were going to sail into summer seas. And that must be warm and pleasant water. Don't you think so?"

Rose was looking over the rail now. She pointed.

"That doesn't look as though the water was warm," she cried. "See the lumps of ice, Russ? It must be ice water. Where do you suppose the summer seas are?"

"We are going to them," declared her brother with confidence.

"Daddy said so. He said we would go out to a place he called the Gulf Stream and that the water would be warm there and the air would be warmer, too."

"What do you think of that?" gasped Rose. "A stream in an ocean? I guess he was joking."

"Oh, no, he wasn't. He said it real serious. He told Aunt Jo about it."

"But how can a stream - that means a river - be running in the ocean? There wouldn't be any banks!" declared the doubtful Rose.

"Let's go and ask him about it," suggested Russ. "And we'll want to keep on the lookout for that Gulf Stream too. I wouldn't want to go past it without seeing it."

They were just about to hunt for Daddy Bunker in the crowd on deck when Laddie came running to them. He was very much excited and he could hardly speak when he reached his older brother and sister.

"Oh! Oh! Oh!" gasped the smaller boy.

"What is the matter, Laddie?" demanded Russ.

"If it is another riddle, Laddie, take your time. We'll stop and listen to it."

"It isn't a riddle - Yes, it is, too! I guess it's a sort of riddle, anyway," said Laddie. "Have you seen him?"

"That sounds like a riddle," said Rose. "And of course we haven't seen him. What is the answer?"

"Who is it that you are asking your riddle about?" demanded Russ.

"Mun Bun," declared Laddie, breathing very hard, for he had run all the way from the stateroom.

"Mun Bun isn't a riddle," said his sister. "He can't be."

"Well, he's lost," declared Laddie. "We can't find him. He was there one minute, and just the next he was gone. And Mother can't find him, and Vi's gone to hunt for Daddy, and - and - anyhow, Mun Bun has lost himself and we don't any of us know what has become of him."

CHAPTER VI

THE SEA-EAGLE

Mun Bun was not a very disobedient little boy; but as Daddy Bunker said, he had a better "forgetery" than he had memory. Mun Bun quite forgot that Mother Bunker had told him not to leave the bigger stateroom where she was setting things to rights in her usual careful way. For, as they were to be several days on the steamship, she must have a place for things and everything in its place, or she could not comfortably take care of Daddy and six children.

Then, Mun Bun was so quick! Just as Laddie said: one minute he was there, and the next minute he wasn't. He seemed to glide right out of sight. Cowboy Jack had called Mun Bun a blob of quicksilver; and you know you cannot put your finger on a blob of quicksilver, it runs so fast.

That is what Mun Bun had done. Mother Bunker's back was turned; Russ and Rose were on deck; the other three children, the twins and Margy, were busy prying into every corner of the stateroom to "see what it was meant for," when Mun Bun just stepped out.

How long he had been gone when their mother discovered the little boy's absence, of course she did not know. She sent Laddie and Vi flying for help - the one for Russ and Rose and the other for their father. She dared not leave the staterooms herself for fear Mun Bun would reappear and be frightened if he did not find her.

She called loudly for him, without getting any answer. Other passengers began to take an interest in the loss of the little boy. Stewards began to hurry about, looking for a lost boy in the most unlikely places. Some of these cubbyholes were so tiny that a canary bird could scarcely have hidden in them, while other places where the stewards looked would have hidden a giant.

When Mr. Bunker appeared in haste from the smoking cabin, having been found by Vi, Mrs. Bunker fairly cast herself into his arms.

"Oh, Charles!" she cried. "He's fallen overboard!"

"You would never think of such a thing, Amy," returned her husband, "if the ship wasn't entirely surrounded by water."

"How can you joke, Charles?" she cried.

"I don't joke. Do you know how high the bulwarks are? A little boy like Mun Bun could not have fallen overboard. He could not climb the bulwarks."

"I never thought of that," agreed Mother Bunker more cheerfully.

"He might have fallen into one of the holds; but I don't believe he has done even that. And there are so many officers and men going up and down the ladders that I believe he has not even gone off this deck. For somebody would be sure to see him."

"Of course he didn't go ashore again?" suggested Rose, who with the other children had returned to the staterooms.

"Oh, no. We had started - were well down the harbor in fact - before he disappeared."

"Mun Bun is a reg'lar riddle," said Laddie. "He runs away and we can't find him; and we hunt for him and there he ain't. Then he comes back by himself - sometimes."

"Is that a riddle?" asked his twin scornfully.

"We-ell, maybe it will be when I get it fixed right."

"I don't think much of it," declared Violet. "And I want to find Mun Bun."

"Don't you other children get lost on this big ship," said Mother Bunker. "Don't go off this floor."

"You mean deck, don't you, Mother?" asked Russ politely. "Floors are decks on board ship. Daddy said so."

"You'd better go and look for him, Russ; and you, too, Rose," the anxious woman said, as Daddy Bunker strode away. "But you other three stay right here by me. I thought that traveling on the train with you children was sometimes trying; but living on shipboard is going to be worse."

"Yes, Mother," said Rose gravely. "There are so many more places for Mun Bun to hide in aboard this ship. Come, Russ."

The two older Bunker children did not know where to look for their little brother. But Russ had an idea. He usually did have pretty bright ideas, and Rose admitted this fact.

"You know we got up early this morning," Russ said to his sister, "and we have been awful busy. And here it is noontime. Mun Bun doesn't usually have a nap until after lunch, but I guess he's gone somewhere and hidden away and gone to sleep. And when Mun Bun's asleep it is awful hard to wake him. You know that, Rose Bunker."

"Yes, I know it," admitted Rose. "But where could he have gone?"

Russ thought over that question pretty hard. Daddy Bunker would have said that the little lost boy's older brother was trying to put himself in Mun Bun's place and thinking Mun Bun's thoughts.

Now, if Mun Bun had been very sleepy and had crept away to take a nap, as he often did after lunch when they were at home, without saying anything to Mother Bunker about it, where would he have gone to take that nap on this steamboat?

Mun Bun was a bold little boy. He was seldom afraid of anything or anybody. Had he not instantly made friends with Sam, the strange colored boy, at Aunt Jo's house? So Russ knew he would not be afraid to run right out on the deck among the other passengers.

"But that would not be a nice place to go for a nap," said Russ aloud.

"What wouldn't?" asked Rose, quite surprised by her brother's sudden speech.

"Out here on the deck. No, he didn't come out here at all," said Russ, with confidence.

Russ was an ingenious boy, as we have seen. Once having got the right idea in his head he proceeded to think it out.

"Come on back, Rose," he said suddenly, seizing his sister's hand.

"What for?"

"To find Mun Bun."

"But he isn't with Mother!"

"I bet - No, I don't mean that word," said Russ. "I mean I *think* he is with Mother, only she doesn't know it."

Laura Lee Hope

"Why, Russ Bunker, that sounds awfully silly!"

But she followed after him in much haste. They came running to the two staterooms which Daddy Bunker had engaged. Mother and the other children were the center of a group of sympathetic people in the corridor.

"Oh! did you find him?" Rose cried.

"Of course not," said Vi. "Where should we find him?"

"Here," announced Russ, pushing through the crowd.

"Of course he isn't here, Russ," said Vi. "Can't you count us? Mun Bun is not here."

"Well, let me see," said the boy, and he pushed into the bigger stateroom where his mother had been working when Mun Bun disappeared. Then he opened the door between that room and the other room. It was all quiet in there. He glanced into the two berths. There was nobody in either of them.

"You are mistaken, Russ," whispered Rose, looking in at the door he had left open. "He can't be here. Daddy has just come and says the captain has promised to have the ship searched."

But without making any reply Russ Bunker went down on his knees, looked under the lower berth, and then stretched an arm under and grabbed something with his hand.

A sleepy squeal came from under the berth. Russ, laughing, dragged at the chubby ankle his hand had grasped. Mun Bun's cross, sleepy voice was raised in protest:

"Don't you! Don't you! Let me be!"

Mother and Daddy Bunker came running.

"That blessed baby!" cried his mother.

"That pestiferous youngster!" exclaimed his father.

But he smiled happily, too, when Mun Bun was completely drawn out from under the berth by Russ and was in his mother's arms again. She sat down and rocked him to and fro while he "came awake" and looked around at the others.

"You have begun well," said Daddy Bunker gravely. "Stirring up the whole ship's company before we are out of sight of land! I must hurry and tell the captain to call off his sea-dogs. The lost is found."

"What are sea-dogs?" demanded Vi. "Do they have dogs at sea to hunt for lost children - dogs like Alexis?"

Nobody answered that question, but Rose and Russ, trotting along the deck beside their father, were more fortunate in getting their questions answered.

"Are we really going to sail out of sight of land, Daddy?" asked Rose.

"We certainly are," said Mr. Bunker.

"But there is a lot of land," said the girl, pointing. "We can't lose all that, can we?"

"That is just what we are going to do. You watch. By and by the land will be only a line on the horizon, and then it will fade out of sight entirely."

So Russ and Rose remained on deck to watch the land disappear. Rose expected it to go something like a "fade-out" on the moving picture screen. The disappearance of the land proved to be a very long matter, however, and the two children went below for lunch when the first call came.

The purser had arranged for the Bunker family at a side table where they could be as retired as though they were at home.

There were not many other children aboard, and the purser liked children anyway. So between his good offices and that of the colored stewards, the Bunkers were well provided for.

Even the captain - a big, bold-looking man with a gray mustache and lots of glittering buttons on his blue coat - stopped at the Bunker table to ask about Mun Bun.

"So that is the fellow I was going to put about my ship for and go back to Boston to see if he had been left on the dock!" he said very gruffly, but smiling with his eyes at Mun Bun, who smiled back. "He looks like too big a boy to make such a disturbance on a man's ship."

"Oh, I don't think, Captain Briggs, he will do it again," said Mother Bunker.

"I dess wanted to sleep," murmured Mun Bun, holding up his spoon.

"Next time you want your watch below," said Captain Briggs, shaking his head, "you report to me first. Do you hear?"

"Yes, Ma'am," said Mun Bun, quite sure that he had said the right thing although they all laughed at him.

Mother Bunker kept the little fellow close to her thereafter; but Vi and Laddie followed the two older children out on deck. There was a comfortably filled passenger list on the *Kammerboy*; but the wind was rather heavy that afternoon and many of them remained in the cabins. But the four children had a great game of hide and seek all over the forward deck.

Finally Daddy Bunker appeared from aft to make sure that none of the quartette was lost. He took Laddie and Vi below with him after a time and the two older children were left alone. They found seats in the lee of what the ship's men called "the house" and sat down to rest and talk. But every now and then one of them jumped up to look astern to see if the land had disappeared, as Daddy Bunker said it would.

"It's a long time going," said Rose.

"Well, there is a lot of it to go. Don't you remember," said Russ, "how big the North American continent is in the geography?"

"Oh! Is that it?" cried Rose.

"Yes. We've got to lose the whole top part of North America," her confident brother declared.

There was some sort of officer (he had brass buttons and wore a cap, so Russ and Rose knew he must be an officer) pacing the deck, back and forth, not far from their chairs. Every time he came near he threw a pleasant word to the brother and sister. Russ and Rose began to ask him questions and sometimes trotted beside him as he paced his lookout watch. Violet would have delighted in this man, for he seemed to know almost everything about ships and the sea and was perfectly willing to answer questions.

Rose asked him if, after they had lost the land, they would find the Gulf Stream that Daddy Bunker had told them about.

"Pretty soon thereafter, little lady," said the man.

"And - and does it have banks?" pursued Rose.

"Does what have banks?" the man asked, in surprise. "The Gulf Stream?"

"Yes, sir."

"No," chuckled the sailor. "It's not like a river - not just like one."

"Then how do you know when you come to the Gulf Stream?"

Laura Lee Hope

demanded Russ. "I should think you'd sail over it without knowing."

But the sailor told them that the stream, or current, was very broad, that the water was much warmer than the surrounding ocean, and that the Gulf Stream was even a different color from the colder ocean.

"Oh, we won't miss it," declared the man, shaking his head.

Just then Rose saw something out over the ocean, sailing low and making a great flapping of black wings. She pointed eagerly:

"There's a buzzard, Russ - like those we saw in Texas."

"Oh, no, little lady, that isn't a buzzard," said the sailor.

"It must be a gull. There were lots of them back in the harbor, you know, Rose," her brother rejoined.

"And it's not a gull," said the man, squinting his eyes to look at the distant bird. "It's too big. I declare! I think that's an eagle."

"Oh! An eagle like those on top of the flagstaffs?" cried Russ.

"And on the gold pieces?" added Rose, for she had a gold piece that had been given her on her last birthday.

"No, not that kind of eagle," said the man. "But he's related. Yes, sir; it's a sea-eagle; some call 'em, I guess rightly, ospreys. They're fishers, but they can't roost on the sea. That one's a long way off shore. Something is the matter with him."

"Do you suppose he's hungry?" asked Rose doubtfully.

"I shouldn't wonder if hunger drove him out here so far from land," said the sailor, smiling. "But he's been hurt. You can see how his left wing droops. Yes, something has happened to that bird."

The bird beat his way heavily toward the ship. First it rose a little way in the air, and then it slid down as though almost helpless, beating its good wing prodigiously to keep from falling into the water.

"He's making bad weather of it," said the sailor. "Poor chap. If he comes aboard -"

"Oh! we'll feed him and mend his wing," cried Rose. "He's just like - Why, Russ Bunker! that poor bird is just what Aunt Jo called poor Sam, a tramp. That is what he is."

"A sea-going tramp, I guess," said the sailor, laughing.

But he watched the coming sea bird quite as interestedly as did the two children. The creature seemed to have selected the steamship as its objective point, and it beat its good wing furiously so as to get into the course of the *Kammerboy*.

"Can we have the bird if it gets aboard, Mr. Officer?" asked Russ eagerly.

"If I can catch it without killing it - for they are very fierce birds - it shall be yours," promised the man.

At once, therefore, the eagerness and interest of Russ and Rose Bunker were vastly increased. They clung to the rail and watched the approaching bird with anxious eyes. It was coming head on toward the bow of the ship. Would the *Kammerboy* get past so swiftly that the sea-eagle could not reach it?

The uncertainty of this, and the evident effort of the great bird to fly a little farther, greatly excited the two older of the six little Bunkers.

Laura Lee Hope

CHAPTER VII

A SIGNAL OF DISTRESS

The steamship was pursuing her course so swiftly, but so easily, that Russ and Rose Bunker scarcely realized that the chances of the big bird's landing on the craft were very slim. The children raced along the deck toward the bows, believing that the big bird would alight there. Their friend, the lookout officer, however, remained at his post.

The big wings of the great sea-eagle beat the air heavily. They were covered with almost black feathers above while the feathers on the under side of the wings were pearl-gray, a contrast that Rose said was "awfully pretty."

"I don't see anything pretty about that poor, struggling bird," said Russ shortly. "He's hurt bad. I hope he gets here all right, but - Oh! There he goes!"

It was a fact that the big bird almost fell into the sea, being weakened. The bow of the *Kammerboy* swept past the struggling creature. Russ and Rose lifted a joined complaint:

"Oh, he's drowned! He drowned!"

It was true that the bird was not a water-fowl and, as the officer had told the children, could not "roost" on the sea. It was not web-footed, so could not swim. And with an injured wing it was wonderful that it had kept up as long as it had, for it was now far, far from the shore.

But the bird had wonderful courage. Although plunged into the water and suffering one wave to break and pour over him, the great bird sprang into the air once more. He would not give up the fight! Russ and Rose saw the flashing eyes, the hooked beak parted, and every other evidence of the creature's putting forth a last remaining effort to reach a secure resting place for his feet.

And he made it! He beat his powerful wings for the last time and shot up over the rail of the steamship. The children shouted with delight. Other passengers had been attracted to the place. The officer who had made himself the friend of Russ and Rose was prepared for the bird's coming inboard. He ran with a piece of strong netting in his hands, and as the bird came thumping down on the deck, the man cast this net about the creature.

Then what a flapping and croaking and struggling there was! A sailor ran forward with a boat-stretcher and wanted to hit the bird; but Russ and Rose screamed, and the officer sent the man away.

"We're not going to kill the bird. These little folks want it alive," said the officer. "And so we are going to make a prisoner of it and mend that wing if we can."

"Aye, aye, Quartermaster," said the sailor who had tried to interfere.

"See if you can find a big poultry cage," said the officer. "We had live turkeys aboard for the Thanksgiving run, and what would hold a turkey ought to hold a sea-eagle. Lively now!"

"Aye, aye, sir," said the man, and hurried away.

While they waited for the cage the quartermaster warned the two Bunker children to remain well back from the struggling bird, for it might get away.

"He is certainly a strong bird," said one of the other passengers, looking on, too, from a safe distance. "Don't you think he'd better be killed, Officer?"

"Oh, no! Oh, no!" chorused Russ and Rose.

"Of course not. You're one of those folks, sir, that would kill an American eagle, too - the bird that is supposed to represent the best fighting spirit of this country. No, sir! this bird is going to have his chance. If we can heal his wounds, we will set him free again - hey, little folks?"

"Of course we will," said Russ stoutly.

"Yes, sir! we'll set him free," agreed Rose. "But when you do it I am going down to the stateroom. I think he is pretty savage."

It was quite true. The injured bird was savage. But when Daddy Bunker heard about the capture and saw the sea-eagle in its cage, he pointed out the fact that there was good reason for the bird to be savage if it had a broken wing.

"You would be cross if you had a broken arm, Russ," Daddy Bunker said soberly, "So come away and let the poor bird alone for a while. Maybe it will eat and drink if it is not watched so closely."

It was found that a bullet had passed through the fleshy part of the great bird's wing. The quartermaster declared that, without much doubt, the bird had been shot at from a small boat and by some idle and thoughtless "sportsman."

"It is wrong," Daddy Bunker said, "to call such people 'sportsmen.' There is no real sport in shooting at and laming an inoffensive creature, one that cannot be made use of for food. That excuse does not hold in this case."

"True word, sir," said the quartermaster. "It was a wicked trick, I'll say. But I think the bird will recover very shortly. Perhaps the little folks can see the bird released before we get to Charleston."

"Not me!" cried Rose again. "I am going right downstairs when you open that cage and set him free. He has got such a wicked eye."

And truly, interested as she was in the poor bird, Rose Bunker did not often go near him during the time he was in captivity. She found other things to interest her about the swiftly sailing *Kammerboy*.

So did all the other Bunkers. For what interested the six little Bunkers was sure to interest Daddy and Mother Bunker. It just *had* to. As Mother Bunker observed, Mun Bun was not the only one of her flock over whom she must keep pretty close watch.

They were really well behaved children; but mischief seemed to crop up so very easily in their lives. Daddy said that any Bunker could get into more adventures nailed into a wooden cage no bigger than the turkey crate the great sea-eagle was housed in than other children could find in a ten acre lot!

Living at sea on this great steamship was a good deal like living in a hotel. And the little Bunkers had lived in hotels, and liked the fun of it. Traveling by water was even more fun than traveling on a train. The *Kammerboy* was a fine big ship and there was so much to see and to learn that was new and surprising that that first night none of them really wanted to go to bed.

Although even that was a new experience. The staterooms were different from the berths in a sleeping car. Laddie thought they ought all to be tied into their berths so, if the ship rolled, they would not fall out.

"For I don't like falling out of bed," he said. "I always bump myself."

The steamship did not roll that night, however. At least if it did the little Bunkers did not know it. They slept soundly and were up bright and early in the morning and were all dressed and out on deck in the sunshine long before the first breakfast call came.

They made a call on the captive sea-eagle before breakfast and he seemed to be recovering, for he snapped his beak viciously when they drew near and spread his wings as far as the cage would allow.

"I don't think he's very nice," said Rose. "He doesn't seem to know we were kind to him."

"What are you going to do with him, Rose?" asked Vi.

"Let him go when his wing is well."

"But I guess he doesn't know that," said Laddie. "If he did he'd feel better about it."

"He bites," said Mun Bun reflectively. "I'd rather have Alexis. Alexis doesn't bite."

"Alexis would bite if he thought anybody was going to hurt him," said Russ. "But we can't make this eagle understand."

"Why not?" immediately demanded Vi.

"Because we can't talk bird-talk," replied Rose, giggling.

"When I go to school I'll learn bird-talk," announced Mun Bun. "And I'll learn to talk dog-talk and cat-talk, too. Then they'll all know what I mean."

"That is a splendid idea, dear," Rose said warmly. "You do

just that."

"S'posing they don't teach those languages where you go to school, Mun Bun?" suggested Laddie gravely. "I guess they don't in all schools. They don't in the Pineville school, do they, Russ?"

"I'll ask Mother to send me to a school where they do," declared Mun Bun before Russ could reply. "I don't need to learn to talk our kind of talk. I know that already. But birds and dogs and cats are different."

"You talk pretty good, I guess, Mun Bun," said Russ. Mun Bun was quite proud of this. He did not know that he often said "t" for "c" and "w" for "r." "But you will be a long time learning to speak so that this bird could understand."

"Well, I shall try," the littlest Bunker declared confidently.

Anyhow, it was decided that the sea-eagle would have to be released before Mun Bun learned to talk the eagle language. The quartermaster who was Russ and Rose's particular friend, came along with some raw meat scraps for the big bird; but the children had to go to breakfast before the bird gobbled these up. He was very shy.

Later in the forenoon Russ and Rose were walking along the deck near a little house amidships and they heard a funny crackling sound - a crackling and snapping like a fresh wood fire. They stopped and looked all around.

"I don't see any smoke," said Russ. "But there's a fire somewhere."

"What is that mast with the wires up there for, Russ?" asked his sister, looking upward.

"Oh! Daddy told me that was the wireless mast," Russ exclaimed.

"But that can't be," said Rose warmly. "It has wires hitched to it; so it can't be wire *less*."

"You know, Rose, they talk from ship to ship, and to the shore, by wireless."

"What does that mean?" returned the girl. "A telegraph?"

"That's it!" cried Russ. "And I guess that is what the crackling is. Listen!"

"Isn't it a fire, then, that we hear?" for the crackling sound continued.

"That's the electric spark," said her brother eagerly. "That is what it must be. Let's peep into this room, Rose. It is where the telegraph machine is."

There was a window near by, but as they approached it the two children found a door in the wireless house, too, and that door was open. A man in his shirt-sleeves and with a green shade over his eyes and something that looked like a rubber cap strapped to his head was sitting on a bench in front of some strange looking machinery.

He was writing on a pad and the crackling sound came from an electric spark that flickered back and forth in the machine before him. Russ and Rose gazed in, wide-eyed.

At length the crackling stopped and the spark went out with a sputter. The man stopped writing and wheeled about in his seat. He saw them looking in at the doorway.

"Hullo!" he exclaimed. "If here aren't two of the little Bunkers. Do you want to send a message by wireless?"

"Thank you," said Rose promptly. "I think it would be nice to send word to Aunt Jo that we are all right and that the ship is all right and that we caught an eagle."

"It costs money to send messages," said the wiser Russ.

"Oh! Does it?" asked his sister.

"I am afraid it does," replied the operator, laughing. "You had better ask Mr. Bunker about sending a message to your aunt, after all. Some messages we do not charge for. But the rules demand that all private messages must be paid for in advance."

"Well, then, I guess we'd better write a letter to Aunt Jo," said Rose, who was practical, after all. "That won't cost anything but a two cent stamp."

"Oh, my!" laughed Russ. "Going to mail it in the ocean?"

"We'll mail it when we get to Charleston," said Rose cheerfully. "I guess Aunt Jo won't mind."

Just at this moment there seemed to be some excitement on the deck up forward. Two officers who stood on what the children had learned was called the quarter were talking excitedly to one of the lookout men. They were pointing ahead, and one of the officers put a double-barreled glass to his eyes and stared ahead.

The operator came to the doorway of his cabin and looked forward, too. He could see over the bulwarks and marked what had caused the excitement.

"Ah-ha!" he said. "Come up here, little folks, and you can see it too."

Russ and Rose were quite excited. They stepped up into the doorway beside the wireless operator. They both saw at once the two-masted vessel that was rolling sluggishly in the sea. Her rail seemed almost level with the water and from one of the masts several flags were strung.

"What is it?" cried Russ. "That ship looks as though it was

going down."

"I guess you've hit it right. She does look so," said the operator. "She has sprung a leak, sure enough. And she's set distress signals."

"Those flags?" asked Russ. "Do those flags say she is sinking?"

"Those flags ask for help. That schooner doesn't carry a wireless outfit as this vessel does. Few small vessels do. I guess we will have to help her out," said the wireless operator.

CHAPTER VIII

A GREAT DEAL OF EXCITEMENT

Russ and Rose Bunker were very much excited by the discovery of the schooner in distress. They were actually afraid that the vessel was going to sink in the ocean right before their eyes!

But the wireless operator reassured them. He said it probably would not sink at all. He seemed to have learned at first glance a lot about that schooner.

"It's lumber laden, from some Maine port. Probably going to Baltimore, or some port down that way. They have jettisoned her deck load, and now she'll just float soggily. But her sails will never carry her to port."

Russ eagerly asked what "jettisoned" meant, and the man explained that the crew had pushed overboard all the deckload of lumber. The hold was filled with the same kind of cargo, and of course lumber would not really sink. But the dirty, torn sails which the children saw did not promise to hold wind enough to propel the water-logged craft.

"She's got to have help," said the wireless operator, and Russ and Rose realized that the *Kammerboy* was slowing down.

"Are we going to stop?" asked Rose. "Will they take the men off that ship into our small boats? Oh, it's a regular shipwreck, Russ!"

"Not much it isn't, little girl," said the operator. "And this steamer can't stop to do much in the way of rescue. The crew wouldn't want to leave that schooner in good weather, anyway."

"What shall we do, then?" Rose asked again.

Just then their friend, the quartermaster, hurried up with a written paper which he handed to the operator.

"Get that out, Sparks," he said, and the operator turned swiftly to his instrument and fitted on his cap and "earlaps" again. At least, Rose said they were "earlaps."

"Can't we help that schooner?" asked Russ of the quartermaster.

"They don't need us to help them. Only to send a message," was the reply, as the wireless spark began to crackle again. "We are telling the Government about her plight and a revenue cutter will be sent out to tow the schooner into some near port. She has drifted a good way off shore, but the weather is settled and there is nothing to fear."

In a few moments the operator had sent the message and got a reply.

"Right out of the air," breathed Rose wonderingly. "I think that is very funny, Russ. If that mast isn't exactly wireless, it is almost wireless. Anyway, the wires aren't long enough to take much of a message, I should think."

This was a mystery that Russ could not expound, so they went to hunt up Daddy Bunker for further information regarding the wonder of the wireless service. The other four little bunkers were already greatly interested in the deeply rolling lumber schooner.

After more signals with flags had been exchanged between the steamship the children were on and the schooner, the former picked up speed again. Soon the masts of the schooner were almost out of sight; but the little Bunkers continued to discuss the strange incident.

"I wish we could have put out boats and saved them," said Rose. "Like a regular wreck, I mean."

"The crew of the schooner would be castaways, then," Russ mused. "I like to read stories about castaways."

"Robinson Crusoe had goats," remarked Laddie. "I like goats."

"You wouldn't like goats if they butted you, would you?" asked Vi.

"All goats don't butt," said her twin with assurance.

"Have those men got goats on that wabbly schooner?" Margy demanded. "I didn't see any."

"Of course they haven't," Rose replied.

"Then how could they be castaways?" put in Vi promptly. "If castaways have goats -"

"Oh! you don't understand," declared Russ. "They only get the goats after they get to the desert islands. That is what Laddie means."

"Of course," agreed Laddie.

"Do they eat 'em?" Margy asked.

"Only if they need to," Russ told her, with superior wisdom. "Of course, they most always make pets of them."

"Oh!"

"I guess," said Russ, becoming reflective, "that we might play at castaway."

"When we get ashore, do you mean, Russ?" Vi asked.

"Right here."

"No," said Vi. "We'd get our feet wet. We can't play on the ocean, can we?"

"We can play on this deck. The officers won't mind. Now all of you come up on to this life raft. We'll play you are floating around on the sea waiting for somebody to come along in a boat and rescue you."

"Who is going to be the rescuer?" Vi asked.

"I am."

"Are you sure you can rescue us, Russ?" she demanded. "Where's your boat?"

Russ pointed to a long lifeboat covered with canvas which lay some distance from the life-raft. "That will be my boat," he said eagerly. "Rose, you must be in command of the raft. Of course, you have been drifting about a long time and you are all hungry and thirsty."

"Mun Bun wants bwead and milk," put in the littlest Bunker, on hearing this.

"Well," said Laddie soberly, "you've got to want it a lot before you get rescued, Mun Bun. Castaways have to drink the ocean and eat their shoes before anybody rescues them."

At this Mun Bun set up a wail. It seemed that his shoes were brand new and he was very proud of them. He would not consider eating them for a moment!

"Never mind," said Rose, hugging him. "If you get so very hungry before Russ rescues us, you can chew on your belt. That is what Laddie means."

Mun Bun observed his belt with round eyes. It seemed to him, and he confessed it to Rose, that he would have to be awfully hungry to chew that belt. The others entered into the spirit of the play and when Vi chanced to step off the raft her twin and Margy seized her and screamed.

"You'll be drowned, Vi Bunker!" said Margy.

"You'll more than get your feet wet if you don't stay on the raft," her twin scolded. "And, then, maybe there are sharks."

"Sharks?" put in Margy.

"Yes, big sharks."

"What do they do?" asked Margy, who had not heard so much about this castaway play as the older children.

"Big fish," said Laddie promptly.

"I like fish," Margy announced. "You know, Grandma Bell had goldfish. They were pretty."

"And I like fish to eat," said Vi. "Are sharks good to eat?"

"Maybe they will eat you," warned Laddie, who had entered into the play with all his thought and interest.

"Oh, Laddie Bunker! They wouldn't," cried Vi.

"Well, they might. Anyway, you've got to be afraid of the sharks and not step off the raft."

Meanwhile Russ had gone over to the lifeboat. He had not asked even his friend, the quartermaster, if he could play in that boat. But he saw no reason why he could not, as nobody seemed to be using it.

The canvas cover was tied down with many strings; but the knots slipped very easily and the boy pulled out three of the knots and then laid back a corner of the canvas. It was dark inside the boat, and before Russ crept into it as he intended, he bent over the gunwale and peered in.

Suddenly he gasped, and pulled his head back. He was startled, but Russ Bunker was a courageous boy. He had seen something - or he thought he had seen something - squirming in the brown darkness inside the boat.

He waited a little, and then put his head under the canvas and took a long look. Was there something or somebody there? Russ was determined to find out!

CHAPTER IX

RUSS'S SECRET

Russ Bunker looked very funny - Rose said he did - when he suddenly came back to the raft. Vi and Margy shouted to him that he would be drowned; and Laddie said something more about sharks. But their older brother paid little attention to them.

He had tied the cover down over the lifeboat again and he would not look toward it, not even when Rose asked him what the matter was and if he was going to leave all five of the castaways on the raft to starve and be thirsty until luncheon time.

"I guess this isn't a very good place to play castaway, after all," said Russ gravely. "And, anyway," he added, with sudden animation, "there's the man with the gong. We'll have to run down and get cleaned up before we go to the table."

"Dear me!" complained Laddie, "we never can have any fun. We always have to stop and eat or go to bed, or something. Even on this ship we have to."

Laddie thought that the most important thing in the world was play. Rose watched Russ with a puzzled look. She felt that something had happened that her brother did not want to talk about. Russ had a secret.

The latter did not even look again at the lifeboat as the little party passed it on the way to the staterooms. But Russ Bunker's mind was fixed upon that boat and what he had seen in it, just the same. He really could not decide what to do. He was very much puzzled.

Even his mother and father noticed that Russ was rather silent at the lunch table; but he said he was all right. He had something to think about, he told them. Daddy and Mother Bunker looked at each other and smiled. Russ had a way of thinking over things before he put his small troubles before them, and they suspected that nothing much was the matter.

But Rose whispered to her brother before they left the table.

"I think that isn't very polite, Russ Bunker."

Russ looked startled.

"What isn't polite?" he asked almost angrily.

"I saw you do that," she said, in the same admonishing way.

"Do what?" he demanded boldly.

"Put those rolls and the apple in your pocket. You wouldn't do that at home."

"Well, we're not at home, are we?" he said. "You just keep still, Rose Bunker."

Russ ran away directly after he had been excused from the table and they did not find him again for quite a while. He appeared with his usual cheerful whistle on his lips and made up a fine game of hide and seek on the afterdeck. But it was noticeable, if anybody had thought to notice it at all, that Russ kept them all from going near the lifeboat and the raft, and he would not hear to their playing castaway at all.

"Why not?" asked Vi.

"Oh, that's too old," Russ declared. "We can play that at any time. Let's go and listen to the wireless spark. When we get to that plantation where we are going maybe I can set up a wireless mast and we will send messages."

"To Grandma Bell? And to Aunt Jo?" asked Vi.

"Oh!" cried Laddie, "let's send one to Cowboy Jack. I know he'd be glad to hear from us."

So Russ turned the interest of his brothers and sisters away from the castaway play. All but Rose. She wondered just what it was that was troubling Russ and what the lifeboat had to do with it.

But there were so many new things to be interested in aboard the steamship that even Rose forgot to be puzzled after a while. Their friend, the quartermaster, took them all over the ship. They saw the engines working, and peered down into the stoke hole which was very hot and where the firemen worked in their undershirts and trousers and a great clanging of shovels and furnace doors was going on.

"I guess the steampipes always hum on this boat," remarked Laddie. "It is not like it was at Aunt Jo's before that Sam boy came to make the furnace go."

Whether the steampipes hummed or not, the children found that it was quite balmy on the boat. Although a strong breeze almost always blew, it was a warm one. They had long since entered into the Gulf Stream and the warm current seemed to warm the air more and more as the *Kammerboy* sailed southward.

It was only two hours after passing the schooner that was in distress when they "spoke," as the quartermaster called it, the revenue cutter which had been sent to help the disabled vessel, steaming swiftly toward the point of the compass where the schooner was wallowing. Mr. Sparks, as the wireless operator was called, had exchanged messages with the Government vessel and he told the little Bunkers that the lumber schooner would be towed into Hampton Roads, from which the cutter had come.

All this time Russ Bunker stayed away from the covered boat on the hurricane deck. Daddy Bunker, as well as Rose, began to wonder at the boy's odd behavior. When dinner time came, Mr. Bunker watched his oldest son sharply.

"Can I go out on deck again for a while?" asked Russ politely, as he moved back his chair at the end of the meal.

"I don't see why you can't. And Rose too," said their mother. "It is not yet dark. But you other children must come with me."

They had all played so hard that it was no cross for the little ones to prepare for bed. Mun Bun and Margy were already nodding.

When Rose looked about for Russ, he had disappeared again. So had Daddy. They had both slipped out of the saloon cabin without a word.

Russ was hurrying along the runway between the house and the bulwarks, and going forward, when Daddy Bunker came around a corner suddenly and confronted him. Russ was so startled that he almost cried out.

"Let's see what you have in your pockets, Russ," said Mr. Bunker seriously, yet with twinkling eyes. "I noticed that you feared there was going to be a famine aboard this steamer, and that you believe in preparing for it. Let me see the contents of your pockets."

"Oh, Father!" gasped Russ.

"Aren't afraid, are you, Russ?" asked Daddy Bunker. "If you weren't afraid to take the food you needn't be afraid to show it."

"It - it was all mine," said Russ, stammeringly. "I only took what was passed to me."

"I know it," said Daddy. "That is one reason why I want to know the rights of this mystery. I can't have my son starving himself for the sake of feeding a sea-eagle."

"Oh! It isn't the eagle, Daddy."

"What is it, then?"

"It - it isn't an it at all!" exclaimed Russ Bunker and he was so very much worried that he was almost in tears.

"What do you mean?" asked his father.

"I - I can't tell you," Russ faltered. "It isn't about me at all. It's somebody else, and I oughtn't to tell you, Daddy."

CHAPTER X

CHARLESTON AND THE FLEET

A boy hates to tell on another person if he is the right kind of boy. And Russ was the right kind of boy.

Daddy Bunker knew this; so he did not scold. He just said quietly:

"Very well, my boy. If you are mixed up in something of which you cannot tell your father, but which you are sure is all right, then go ahead. I am always ready to advise and help you, but if you are sure you do not need my advice, go ahead."

He turned quietly away. But these words and his cheerful acceptance of Russ' way of thinking rather startled the boy, used as he was to Daddy Bunker's ways. He called after him:

"Daddy! I don't know whether I am right or wrong. Only - only I know somebody that needs this bread and meat because he is hungry. He's *real* hungry. Can't I give it to him?"

"I think that hunger should be appeased first. Go ahead," said Mr. Bunker, but still quite seriously. "Then if you feel that you can come and tell me about it, all right."

At that Russ hurried away, much relieved. Rose came into sight and would have run after him, but Daddy Bunker stopped her.

"Don't chase him now. He has something particular to do, Rose."

"I think that's real mean!" exclaimed Rose. "He's hiding something from me!"

"My!" said Daddy, "do you think your brother should tell you everything he knows or does?"

"Why not?" retorted Rose. "I'm sure, Daddy, he is welcome to know everything I know."

"Are you sure? Moreover, perhaps he does not care to know all your secrets," said Mr. Bunker.

"Anyhow, you must learn, Rose, that other people have a right to their own private mysteries; you must not be inquisitive. Russ has got something on his mind, it is true; but without doubt we shall all know what it is by and by."

"Well!" exclaimed Rose, with almost a gasp. She could not quite understand her father's reasoning.

Russ Bunker appeared after a while, looking still very grave indeed for a boy of his age. Daddy kept from saying or doing anything to suggest that he was curious; but Rose found it hard not to tease her brother to explain his taking food from the table and hiding it in his pockets.

"Of course he can't eat it," she whispered to herself. "And he doesn't give it to the eagle. Who ever heard of an eagle eating pound cake with raisins and citron in it? And I saw Russ take a piece of that.

"But he didn't eat much himself. I wonder if he is sick and is hiding it from Mother and Daddy?"

She watched her brother very closely. After a time he seemed more cheerful, and they ran races on the open deck. They knew many of the passengers by this time to speak to. And there were some few other children of about their own ages, too. They talked with these other boys and girls, found out where they lived when they were at home, and learned where they were going to, when they left the *Kammerboy* at Charleston or Savannah.

Just the same Rose knew that her brother was disturbed in his mind. Daddy Bunker's words to her had been sufficient, and Rose said nothing. But she began to believe that she should sympathize with Russ instead of being vexed with him. He did look so serious when he was not talking.

The evening wore on. The moon rose and silvered the almost pond-like sea through which the *Kammerboy* steamed. Even the children were impressed by the beauty of the seascape. Far, far away against the rising moon appeared a fairylike ship sailing across its face, each spar and mast pricked out as black as jet.

"Just like those silhouettes Aunt Jo cut out for us," declared Rose. "Did you ever see anything so cute?"

Russ didn't have much to say about it. He was very grave again. Bedtime came, and the brother and sister went below. The little folks, Margy and Mun Bun, were in the first stateroom with Mother. Already the twins were fast asleep in the second stateroom. Rose was going to sleep with Vi in the lower berth and Russ was to crawl in beside Laddie in the upper.

But Russ did not seem in a hurry to undress and go to bed. Mother brushed Rose's hair for her and the girl got ready for bed in the larger stateroom. When she went into the other room there was Russ sitting on the stool with only his jacket off.

"Why, Russ Bunker! aren't you going to bed to-night?" demanded Rose.

"I suppose so," admitted Russ.

"Well, you'd better hurry. I want you to put out the light. How do you suppose we can sleep?"

Russ reached up and snapped out the electric bulb as Rose threw aside her bath-gown and hopped into bed beside her sister.

"You can't see to undress in the dark, Russ," scolded Rose.

Russ did not say a word. He got up and walked into his mother's and father's stateroom, and greatly to his sister's vexation he closed the door between the two rooms.

Daddy Bunker had just come in.

"Why, Russ," said he, "haven't you gone to bed yet?"

"No, sir," said Russ. "And I guess I can't. I've got to talk to you first. I guess I can't go to sleep till I've told you something."

Daddy smiled at Mother Bunker but nodded to Russ.

"All right," he said. "We will go out on deck again and take a turn up and down and you shall tell me all about it."

Mother made no objection, although the hour was getting late, and she smiled, too, when she saw Russ slip into his jacket again and follow his father out of the stateroom. On the deck Russ burst out with:

"I promised I wouldn't tell anybody. But when I gave him his supper I told him I'd just have to tell my father, I was afraid; and he said he didn't have any father and he didn't know whether fathers wouldn't 'snitch,' and I said my father wouldn't."

"I see," said Mr. Bunker gravely. "You recommended me as being a safe person to trust a secret with. I am glad you did so."

"Yes, sir. For you see he's got to be fed until we get to Charleston."

"Do you mind telling me who this new friend of yours is, and where he is, and why he must be fed?"

"He's a sailor boy. He belongs on a destroyer and got left at Boston when his ship started for Charleston two days ago."

"He is in the Navy?" exclaimed Mr. Bunker, in surprise.

"Yes, sir. And he spent all his money and did not know how to get down there where the fleet will be in winter quarters, he says, unless he went secretly on one of these steamers."

"He is stealing his passage, then?" asked Daddy Bunker.

"I suppose he is, Daddy," said Russ, ruefully enough. "He is in a boat, all covered up with canvas. Up there on the deck. I can show you. I found him quite by myself, and I was sorry for him, 'specially when he said he didn't have anything to eat. And he said, would I keep still about it? And at first I said I would."

"I see," said Daddy Bunker, smiling. "Then you thought that you ought not to keep the secret from me?"

"That's it, Daddy."

"Quite right," rejoined Mr. Bunker encouragingly. "It is not good policy to keep secrets from your mother and father. What do you want to do about it now?"

"Why - why, I want you to tell me," confessed Russ. "I got him some food."

"I see you did," returned his father, smiling. "At your own cost, Russ."

"We-ell, yes, I could have eaten more if I hadn't taken what I did for the sailor boy."

"We'll have to see about that -"

"I don't mind - much. I'm not very hungry," said Russ hurriedly. "It wasn't that made me tell you."

"I know it wasn't, Russ," said Daddy Bunker, with a pride that the little boy did not understand, and he dropped an approving hand upon Russ' shoulder. "Now, I will tell you what we will do. This sailor boy shall have his chance to rejoin his ship without getting into any more trouble than is necessary. He is probably very young and foolish."

"He isn't very old, I guess," said Russ. "He has been in the Navy only a little while, and it was his first 'shore leave,' he called it, in Boston. He had some cousins there. They begged him to stay longer than he should have. And so he got left."

"I'll fix it if I can," promised Daddy Bunker. "Of course, the first thing to do is to pay his fare and then he can come out of the lifeboat and have his proper meals. I will see the purser, and the captain if it is necessary, and you go to bed, Russ."

"That will be nice!" cried the boy, greatly relieved. "Of course I ought to have told you right at first. You always do know how to straighten things out, Daddy!"

"That is what fathers and mothers are for," replied Mr. Bunker. "Go down and go to sleep, Son, and I will do my best for this young deserter."

When Mr. Bunker entered the stateroom an hour later Mother Bunker wanted to know all about it, of course. And if Russ had known just what they both said of him he would certainly

Laura Lee Hope

have been proud.

"He's a manly boy," said Daddy Bunker in conclusion. "I am glad he is our son."

The trouble about it all was, in Rose's opinion, that she never quite understood it. If Russ had done anything to be punished for, he certainly didn't seem to mind the punishment! And Daddy and Mother seemed to have a little secret between them, as well as Russ.

"I don't like secrets," she complained the next day, on thinking it all over.

"Oh, I do!" cried Laddie. "'Specially now that Christmas is coming."

But Rose knew this was not a Christmas secret. She wondered where the nice, pleasant-faced sailor boy came from who seemed to know Russ and Daddy Bunker so well. She had not seen him before. And that was another mystery that nobody seemed willing to explain to her.

They all had so many good times on the *Kammerboy*, however, that Rose really could not be vexed for long. It proved, as had been announced in Boston, that the ship sailed into summer seas. There was scarcely a cloud in sight for the entire voyage, and certainly the steamship did not roll.

At length, late one afternoon, the children were taken up on the hurricane deck to see the islands of Charleston Harbor ahead. Many warships, and of all sizes, lay in the roadstead, but they did not see much of these vessels save their lights that evening.

The *Kammerboy* was docked to discharge freight and some of her passengers. Daddy Bunker arranged for the boy lost from the destroyer to be put aboard his ship. Russ hoped that he would not be punished very sorely for being left behind.

CHAPTER XI

THE MEIGGS PLANTATION

The Bunker children watched the lights of the fleet until quite late in the evening and thought the sight very pretty indeed. They would have liked to have gone aboard at least one of the Government vessels preferably, of course, the one to which their sailor friend belonged, but there was no opportunity for such a visit. For early the next morning the *Kammerboy* steamed out of the harbor of Charleston again on the last lap of her voyage to Savannah.

"You can't do it, Russ - ever!" declared Rose, with confidence.

"Well," said the oldest of the six little Bunkers, puffing very much, "I can try, can't I? I do wish I could cut that pigeon wing just as Sam did it."

They were on the sunshiny deck of the *Kammerboy*, which was plowing now toward the headlands near Savannah Harbor. But the little folks had been seeing the blue line of the shore ever since leaving Charleston, so they were not much interested in it. As Laddie said, they knew it was there, and that was enough.

"We know the continent of North America didn't get lost while we were out there in the Gulf Stream," said the boy twin, with satisfaction. "So it doesn't matter what part of it we hit - it will be land!"

"If we hit it most any old place," said Vi, "we would be shipwrecked and be castaways like the game we started to play that time and Russ wouldn't let us finish. I wonder why?"

She had ended with a question. But Laddie could not answer it. He was watching Russ trying to do that funny dance.

"Uncle Sam's nephew could do it fine," Laddie said to Russ. "But you don't get the same twist to it."

"Me do it! Me do it!" cried Mun Bun excitedly, and he began to try to dance as Russ had. He looked so cunning jumping about and twisting his chubby little body that they all shouted with laughter. But Mun Bun thought they were admiring his dancing.

"Me did it like Sam," he declared, stopping to rest.

"You do it fine, Mun Bun," Russ said.

It was a fact, however, that none of them could cut that pigeon wing as Sam, the colored boy, had cut it in Aunt Jo's kitchen in Boston.

Now that they were nearing the end of the voyage there were many things besides pigeon wings to interest the little Bunkers. In the first place the big sea-eagle had to be released from the turkey coop. The quartermaster called him Red Eye. And truly his eye was very red and angry all the time. And he clashed his great beak whenever anybody came near him.

"I guess you couldn't tame him in a hundred years," Russ said thoughtfully. "He can't be tamed. That is why we have an eagle for a symbol, I guess. We can't be tamed."

It was decided to let Red Eye out of the cage when the ship entered Savannah Harbor.

"He's come a long way with us. He has come away down here

to Georgia," said Rose thoughtfully. "If he lives in Maine, do you s'pose he will ever find his way back?"

"If he doesn't, what matter? It's a fine country," said the quartermaster.

"But he will want to see his relations," said the little girl. "Maybe he's got a wife and children. He will be dreadfully lonesome away down here."

"Maybe you had better take him back with you on the *Kammerboy*," said Russ thoughtfully, to the quartermaster.

But the officer could not do that. There had been some objection made already to the big sea-eagle caged on deck. Besides, the bird's wing was better, and if he was kept much longer confined, the quartermaster said, he might forget how to fly!

So they all gathered around (but at a good distance from the cage you may be sure), and the eagle was released. He had to be poked out of the cage, for it seemed as though he could scarcely believe that the door was open and he was free.

He stalked out upon the deck, his great claws rattling on the planks. He turned his head from side to side, and then opened his beak and, so Vi said, he hissed at them!

"At any rate," admitted Russ afterward, "he did make a funny noise."

"He was clearing his throat," said Laddie, with scorn of his twin. "How could an eagle hiss? He isn't a goose."

Laddie knew all about geese, for Grandma Bell had geese. But he did not know all about eagles, that was sure! Whether Red Eye hissed, or growled, or whatever he did in his throat, he certainly showed little friendliness. He raised his wings and flapped them "to see if they worked right." Then he uttered a decided croak and jumped a little way off the deck.

Evidently this decided him that he was really free and that his great wings would bear him. He leaped into the air again, spreading his wings, and wheeled to go over the stern of the steamship. The spread of his wings when he flapped them was greater than most of the onlookers had supposed.

"Oh! Oh! Look out, Laddie!" shouted Rose.

Her warning came too late. The end of the great pinion swept Laddie off his feet! He went rolling across the deck, screaming lustily.

"Oh! I'm going overboard! Daddy!" he cried.

But it was Russ who grabbed him and stood him on his feet again.

"You're not going overboard at all," said the older brother. "You couldn't. You'd have to climb over the rail to do it."

"We-ell!" breathed Laddie. "It's a wonder he didn't take me right with him!"

Then he, like everybody else, became interested in the passage of the great bird as it mounted skyward. It went up in a long slant at first, and then began to spiral upward, right toward the sun, and presently was out of sight.

"It can look the sun straight in the face," said Daddy Bunker. "Which is something we cannot do."

"No wonder its eye is red, then," said Rose.

"I guess it's sunburnt," said Margy. "I got sunburnt at Captain Ben's."

That night they docked at Savannah and went to a hotel in

two taxicabs, for one would not hold all the Bunkers and their baggage too. The hotel was a nice one, and Rose thought the negro waiters and chambermaids very attentive and very pleasant people.

"They are the smilingest people I ever saw," she confessed to Mother Bunker. "I guess they are thinking of funny things all the time."

"Perhaps," granted her mother. "But they are trained to politeness. And you children must be just as polite."

They all tried to be polite, and Russ grew quite friendly with one of the bellboys who brought them ice water. He asked that boy if he knew how to cut the pigeon wing, and the boy grinned very broadly.

"I sure does!" he declared. "But if the boss heard of me doin' it around dishyer hotel, he'd bounce me."

"Are you made of rubber?" asked Vi, who was standing by.

"What's dat?" he demanded, rolling his eyes. "Is I made of rubber? Course I isn't. I's made of flesh and blood and bones, same as you is, little Miss. Only I isn't w'ite like you is."

"But you said the man would bounce you. Rubber balls bounce," explained Vi.

At that the bellboy went away laughing very heartily, but Vi could not understand why. And, of course, as usual, nobody could explain it to Vi's satisfaction.

"I know a riddle!" cried Laddie, after a moment. "What looks like a boy, but bounces like a rubber ball? Why! A bellboy!"

And he was highly delighted at this and went around telling everybody his new riddle.

Laura Lee Hope

In the morning Mr. Frane Armatage appeared at the hotel and was shown up to the Bunker rooms. Mr. Armatage, as the little Bunkers knew, was an old school friend of Daddy Bunker's; but one whom he had not seen for a long time.

"Why," said Mr. Armatage, who was a slender man with graying hair and a darker mustache, "Charley was only a boy when I last saw him." He was a very jovial man, and red-faced. Rose thought him handsome, and told Mother Bunker so. "No, Charley was only a sapling then. And look at him now!"

"And look at the sprouts that have sprung from that sapling," laughed Daddy Bunker, with a sweeping gesture towards the six little Bunkers.

"Was he only as big as I am?" Russ asked.

"Well, no, come to think of it; he was some bigger than you. We were graduating from college when we parted. But it seems a long time ago, doesn't it, Charley?"

Daddy Bunker agreed to that. Then he and Mr. Armatage talked business for a while. The owner of the Meiggs Plantation wished to get more land and hire more hands for the next year, and through Mr. Bunker he expected to obtain capital for this. Aside from business the two old friends desired very much to renew their boyhood acquaintance and have their wives and children become acquainted.

"I've got half as many young ones as you have, Charley," said Mr. Armatage. "You've beat me a hundred per cent. I wonder if we keep on growing if the ratio will remain the same?"

Russ knew what "ratio" meant, and he asked: "How can it keep that way if we grow to be seven little Bunkers? You can't have three and a half little Armatages, you know."

"That's a smart boy!" exclaimed the tall man, smiling. "He can see through a millstone just as quick as any boy I know. We'll hope that there will be no half-portions of Armatages. I want all my children to have the usual number of limbs and body."

"If you have little girls, and one was only half a little girl," said Rose, "she would be worse off than a mermaid, wouldn't she?"

"She certainly would," agreed the planter.

"Why?" demanded Vi, who did not understand.

"Because half of her would be a fish," said Russ, laughing. "And you would have to have all your house under water, Mr. Armatage, or the mermaid could not get up and down stairs."

"I declare, Charley!" exclaimed the visitor, "these young ones of yours are certainly blessed with great imaginations. I don't believe our children ever thought of such things."

The next day the party went out to the Meiggs Plantation. It was a two-hours' ride on a branch railroad and a shorter and swifter ride in an automobile over the "jounciest" road the children had ever ridden on, for part of the way led through a swamp and logs were laid down side by side to keep the road, as Mr. Armatage laughingly said, from sinking quite out of sight.

But the land on which the Armatage home stood was high and dry. It was a beautiful grassy knoll, acres in extent, and shaded by wide-armed trees which had scarcely lost any leaves it seemed to the little Bunkers, though this was winter. On the wide, white-pillared veranda a very handsome lady and two little girls and a little boy stood to receive the party.

The children did not come forward to greet the visitors, or even their father, until the latter spoke to them. Mr. and Mrs. Bunker were quite sure by the actions of Phillis and Alice and Frane, Junior, that they were not granted the freedom of speech and action that their little ones enjoyed. Mother Bunker pitied those children from the start!

But what amazed the six little Bunkers more than anything else was the number of colored children hanging about the veranda to see the newcomers. Rose confided to Russ that she thought there must be a colored school near by and all the children were out for recess.

And there were so many house-servants that smiling black and brown faces appeared everywhere.

"I guess," said Rose to her mother, "that there must be an awful lot of work to do in this big house. It's lots bigger than Aunt Jo's or Grandma Bell's. It's like a castle, and all these servants are like retainers. I read about retainers in a story. Only these retainers aren't dressed in uniforms."

CHAPTER XII

MAMMY JUNE

From the very beginning, although they said nothing about it even to each other, the six little Bunkers found the three little Armatages "funny." "Funny" is a word that may mean much or little, and often the very opposite of humorous. In this case the visitors from the North did not understand Phillis and Alice and Frane, Junior. They were not like any boys and girls whom the Bunkers had ever known before.

Phillis was twelve - quite a "grown up young lady" she seemed to consider herself. Yet she broke out now and then in wild, tomboyish activities, racing with Russ and Frane, Junior, climbing fences and trees, and riding horses bareback in the home lot. It seemed as though Phil, as they called her, "held in" just as long as she could, trying to put on the airs of grownups, and then just had to break out.

"If you tell mother I did this I'll wish a ha'nt after you!" she would say to her brother, who was the age of Vi and Laddie, and her sister Alice, who was two years younger than herself, but no bigger than Rose. Alice had a very low, sweet, contralto voice, like Mrs. Armatage, and a very demure manner. Rose became friendly with Alice almost at once.

And the way they treated the colored children of their own age and older was just as strange as anything else about the three Armatages. They petted and quarreled with them; they expected all kinds of service from them; and they were on their part, constantly doing things for the children of "the quarters" and giving them presents. Wherever the white children went about the plantation there was sure to be a crowd of colored boys and girls tagging them.

After the first day Mother Bunker was reassured that nothing could happen to her brood, because there were so many of the colored men about the grounds to look after them. As in the house, a black or brown face, broadly a-smile, was likely to appear almost anywhere.

The quarters, as the cabins occupied by the colored people were called, were not far from the house, but not in sight of it. Even the kitchen was in a separate house, back of the big house. After bedtime there was not a servant left in the big house unless somebody was sick.

"Mammy used to live here," Mrs. Armatage explained, in her languid voice, "while the children were small. I couldn't have got along without mammy. She was my mammy too. But she's too old to be of much use now, and Frane has pensioned her. She has her own little house and plot of ground and if her boy - her youngest boy - had stayed with her, mammy would get along all right. She worries about that boy."

The Bunker children did not understand much about this until, on the second day after their arrival, Phillis said:

"I'm going down to see mammy. Want to come?"

"Is - isn't your mammy here at home?" asked Vi. "Dora Blunt calls her mother 'mammy'; but we don't."

"I've got a mother and a mammy too," explained the oldest Armatage girl. "You-all come on and see her. She'll be glad to see you folks from the North. She will ask you if you've seen her Ebenezer, for he went up North. We used to all call him 'Sneezer,' and it made him awfully mad."

"Didn't he have any better name?" asked Russ.

"His full name is Ebenezer Caliper Spotiswood Meiggs. Of course, their name isn't really Meiggs, like the plantation; but the darkies often take the names of the places where they were born. Sneezer was a real nice boy."

"He isn't dead, is he?" asked Russ.

"Reckon not," said Phillis. "But Mammy June is awful' worried about him. She hasn't heard from him now for more than a year. So she doesn't know what to think."

"But she has got other folks, hasn't she?" Rose asked.

"You'd think so! Grandchildren by the score," replied the older Armatage girl, laughing. "Sneezer had lots of older brothers and sisters, and they most all have married and live about here and have big families. The grandchildren are running in and out of mammy's cabin all the time. I have to chase 'em out with a broom sometimes when I go down there. And they eat her pretty near up alive!"

Even the smaller Bunkers knew that this was a figure of speech. The grandchildren did not actually eat Mammy June, although they might clean her cupboard as bare as that of Old Mother Hubbard.

They followed a winding, grass-grown cart path for nearly half a mile before coming to Mammy June's house. The way was sloping to the border of a "branch" or small stream - a very pretty brook indeed that burbled over stones in some places and then had long stretches of quiet pools where Frane, Junior, told Russ and Laddie that there were many fish - "big fellows."

"I'll get a string and a bent pin and fish for them," said Laddie confidently. "I fished that way in the brook at Pineville."

"Huh!" said Frane Armatage, Junior, in scorn. "One of these

Laura Lee Hope

fish here would swallow your pin and line and haul you in."

"Oh!" gasped Vi, with big eyes. "What for?"

"No, the fish wouldn't!" declared Laddie promptly.

"Yes, it would. And swallow you, too."

"No, the fish wouldn't," repeated Laddie, "for I'd let go just as soon as it began to tug."

"Smartie!" said Phillis to her brother. "You can't fool these Bunker boys. Let Laddie alone."

Of course the troop of white children, walking down the cart path to Mammy June's, was followed by a troop of colored children. The latter sang and romped and chased about the bordering woods like puppies out for a rample. Sometimes they danced.

"Can you cut a pigeon wing?" Russ asked one of the older lads. "I want to learn to do that."

"No, I can't do that. Not good. We've got some dancers over at the quarters that does it right well," was the reply.

"You ought to've seen Sneezer do it!" cried another of the colored children. "Sneezer could do it fine. Couldn't he, Miss Phil?"

"Sneezer was a great dancer," admitted the oldest Armatage girl. "Come on, now, Bunkers, and see Mammy June. Keep away from this cabin," she added to the colored children, "or I'll call a ha'nt out of the swamp to chase you."

"I wonder what those 'ha'nts' are, Russ," whispered Rose to her brother. "Do they have feathers? Or don't they fly? They must run pretty fast, for Phil is always saying she will make one chase folks."

"I asked Daddy. There isn't any such thing. It's like we say 'ghosts.'"

"Oh! At Hallowe'en? When we dress up in sheets and things?"

"Yes. Maybe these colored children believe in ghosts. But of course we don't!"

"No-o," said Rose thoughtfully. "Just the same I wouldn't like to think of ha'nts if I was alone in the woods at night. Would you, Russ?"

Russ dodged that question. He said:

"I don't mean to be alone in the woods around here at night. And neither do you, Rose Bunker."

Of course neither of them had the least idea what was going to happen to them before they started North from the Meiggs Plantation.

Mammy June's cabin was of white-washed logs, with vines climbing about the door that were leafless now but very thrifty looking. There were fig trees that made a background and a windbreak for the little house, and a huge magnolia tree stood not far from the cabin. The front door opened upon a roofed porch, and an old colored woman of ample size, in a starched and flowered gingham dress and with a white turban on her head, was rocking in a big arm chair on this porch when the children appeared.

"Lawsy me!" she exclaimed, smiling broadly to show firm white teeth in spite of her age. "Is this yere a celebration or is it a parade? Miss Philly, you got a smooch on dat waist, and your skirt is hiked up behind. I declar' I believe you've lost a button."

"Why, so I have, Mammy June," answered Phillis. "And more than one. Nobody has time to keep buttons sewed on up at the house, now that you're not there."

"Shiftless, no-count critters, dem gals up dere. Sho, honey! who is all dese lil' white children?"

"Bunkers," explained Frane, Junior.

"What's dem?" asked Mammy June, apparently puzzled. "Is dey to play with, or is dey to eat? Bunkers! Lawsy!"

Rose giggled delightedly.

"They are to play with," laughed Alice suddenly. "That is what they are for, Mammy June."

"You see you play pretty with them, then," said the old woman, shaking her head and speaking admonishingly.

Rose and Russ Bunker at least began to understand that this pleasant old colored woman had had the chief care of the three young Armatages while they were little. Perhaps she had trained them quite as much as their mother and father. And they seemed to love Mammy June accordingly.

That the old woman loved little folks and knew how to make friends with them was soon apparent. She had Mun Bun and Margy both together in her ample lap while Laddie and Vi leaned against her and listened to the tale she was telling the little folks.

Phillis and Alice meanwhile showed Rose the interior of the cabin and all its comforts and wonders. Meanwhile Frane, Junior, took Russ down to the stream with some of the colored children to show him some of the big fish he had threatened Laddie with. Here it was that Russ Bunker engaged in his first adventure at the Meiggs Plantation.

CHAPTER XIII

THE CATFISH

"If Sneezer was here," said Frane, Junior, "he'd show you more fish than I can. Sneezer used to just smell 'em out. But come on. I know where some of the big ones stay."

"I don't want to dive in after them," declared Russ Bunker, laughing. "The way you promised Laddie. And I haven't any hook and line at all."

"We won't go fishing. Not really. Mostly the darkies fish. We don't bother to. They bring us plenty to eat when we want them at the house."

"You - you don't do much of anything, do you?" asked Russ doubtfully. "Not for yourselves, I mean."

"Don't have to," returned Frane, Junior. "The darkies do it all for us. But Phil and Alice and I have to do our own studying."

Russ saw that he was in fun, but he was curious enough to ask the smaller boy:

"Do you and the girls go to school?"

"School comes to us. There is a teacher comes here. Lives at the house. But it's vacation time now till after New Year's. I hope she never comes back!"

"Oh, is she mean to you?"

"Course she is," declared Frane, Junior. "She makes us study. I hate to."

"Well, sometimes I don't like what they make us learn in school," admitted Russ slowly. "But I guess it's good for us."

"How do you know, it is?" demanded the other. "I don't feel any better after I study. I only get the headache."

Russ could not find an immediate answer for this statement. Besides, there was something right in front of him then that aroused his interest. It was a big log spanning the stream, with a shaky railing nailed to it, made of a long pole attached to several uprights.

"That is the funniest bridge I ever saw," he declared. "Will it hold you?"

"Look at that log. It would hold a hundred elephants," declared Frane, Junior, who was inclined to exaggerate a good deal at times.

"Not all at once!" cried Russ.

"Yes, sir. If you could get 'em on it," said Frane. "But I don't s'pose the railing would stand it."

When the boys went out on the bridge and Russ considered the railing he was very sure that this last statement of his little friend was true, whether any others were or not. The railing "wabbled" very much, and Russ refrained from leaning against it.

"Now, you folks keep back!" whispered Frane shrilly to the colored children who had followed them. "I want to show him the big fellow that sleeps down here."

Somewhere he had picked up a piece of bark more than a foot long, which was rolled into a cylinder. He lay down on the log near the middle of the brook and began to look down into the brown and rather cloudy water through this odd spyglass.

"What can you see through that thing?" asked Russ.

"Sh! Wait. Don't let 'em hear you," warned Frane, Junior. Then he added: "Get down here 'side o' me. When I spot him I'll let you squint through this too."

Russ understood now that his companion was trying to see one of the fish that lived in the stream - perhaps the "big fellow" Frane had spoken of. Russ grew quite excited and he took off his jacket and rolled up his sleeves. He knelt down beside Frane, and finally lay right down on his stomach and likewise peered over the side of the log.

The log-bridge had been made quite flat on its upper surface with a broadaxe, and all the bark had long since worn off. It was all of thirty feet long, but it was just as firm as the arch of a stone bridge.

"There!" whispered Frane. "I saw a flicker then. Yep! He's there! Right below the edge of that stone!"

"I don't see anything but water. I can't even see the bottom," observed Russ, in a low voice, too.

"Don't you see him below the stone?"

"I don't even see the stone," complained Russ.

"Hush! He'll hear you. I see his tail wiggle. He's a big cat."

"Now, don't tell me there's a cat in this brook!" said Russ Bunker, shortly. "I know there isn't anything of the kind. Cats hate water."

He had already learned that Frane, Junior, was apt to exaggerate. Russ thought the Armatage boy was letting his fancy run wild at this present moment.

"It is a cat," murmured Frane. "I can see his whiskers moving. Yep, a big fellow! Want to see?" and he took his eye away from the bark cylinder.

"Can you see his teeth and his claws and his fur and his tail?" demanded Russ scornfully, and without offering to take the cylinder. He did not intend to be fooled so easily.

"What are you talking about?" hissed Frane. "And speak quietly. You'll drive him away."

"Cats aren't so easily scared," said Russ. "You have to peg stones at 'em to drive 'em away."

"Huh!" sniffed Frane. "Funny cats up North. I don't believe you have any up there."

"You're right we don't," agreed Russ, and now he laughed again. "Not any cats that swim. Cats hate the water - - "

"Aw, shucks! I'm not talking about cats!" exclaimed Frane. "I'm talking about catfish."

"Oh!" ejaculated the Northern boy.

"You know a catfish, don't you? It has feelers that we call whiskers. Awful nice eating, for they only have a backbone."

"Oh!" murmured Russ again. "I guess I didn't understand. Let me see the fish, will you, please?"

"You can look," said Frane passing him the cylinder of bark. "But maybe we have scared him off, talking so much."

The big catfish, however, had not been scared away. After a

few moments, and with Frane's aid, Russ Bunker got the wooden spyglass focused on the proper point. He saw the imbedded rock Frane had spoken of. Then he saw the fish basking in the water below the rock's edge.

It was almost two feet long, with a big head and goggle eyes, and the "whiskers" Frane had spoken of wriggled back and forth in the slow current. Russ grew excited.

"Why!" he whispered to Frane, "I could grab it, if I tried. It is just like what we call bullheads up in Pineville. I've caught 'em in our pond. You can hardly get 'em off the hook without getting stung by 'em."

"Catfish don't sting you. But you have to knock 'em in the head when you land them, so as to make 'em behave. I've seen the boys do it."

"I'm going to make a grab for that fellow," declared Russ.

"I reckon you'd miss him. You couldn't hold him, anyway," said Frane doubtfully.

"I could so."

"No, you couldn't. He's too big. They never catch catfish that way."

"I know I never caught a bullhead that way," admitted Russ. "But one never lay so still for me. And right under this log! Here! You take the spyglass."

"You'd better take care," advised the Southern boy.

But Russ felt very daring. It seemed that the fish lay only a few inches under the surface of the brown water. If he could grasp the fish and throw it ashore, how the other children would all shout! Perhaps Russ Bunker wanted to "show off" a little. Anyway, he determined to make the attempt to land the big catfish with his hands.

"You can't do it," warned Frane, Junior, creeping back a way so as to give Russ more room.

"Don't say that till you see," returned the boy from the North. "Now, look! I know just where he lies. Look!"

Russ had rolled his shirtsleeve up to his shoulder. He balanced himself on the log, his head and shoulders overhanging the brown water. Suddenly he made a dive with his right hand. Even his head touched the water, he dipped so deep, and his cap went floating away.

And, wonderful to relate, his hand did seize upon the catfish. Perhaps the fish had been asleep down there by the edge of the imbedded stone. At any rate it was not quick enough to escape Russ Bunker's darting hand.

"I got it!" yelled Russ, in delight.

He tried to seize fast hold upon the body of the catfish, but the fish shot forward with a wriggle that slapped its tail against Russ's hand. Russ plunged forward, trying to hold it.

"I - guess - he's - a - butter - fish!" he gasped. "He's so slippery -"

And then, losing his balance on the log, Russ Bunker fell right into the deep pool with splash enough to frighten all the fishes for yards around!

CHAPTER XIV

MAMMY JUNE HELPS

Of course, Russ Bunker should not have done it. He was always ready to try new things and wasn't much afraid of anything that turned up. But trying to catch a big catfish with his hands was ridiculous.

Perhaps he realized this when he fell off the log into the stream; but it was too late then to know how foolish it was.

The chorus of screams from the children on the bank was the first announcement that Mammy June had of the mischief that was afoot. The colored children shouted and Frane, Junior, ran right off the log and came screaming to the cabin:

"He's gone down! He's gone down!"

"What is the matter with you, Frane?" demanded the old woman, coming heavily down off the porch. "Who's gone down? Wha's he gone down to?"

"Russ has gone down," announced Frane. "He's gone down after the catfish."

"Lawsy me!" exclaimed Mammy June. "Is that li'le boy got into the branch?"

Rose and Vi and Laddie and Margy and Mun Bun, as well as

the two Armatage girls, all came running, too. For the first minute none of them understood what had happened to Russ.

But when they reached the bank of the stream they saw something splashing in the middle of the pool under the bridge. They couldn't see Russ, but they knew that something was struggling there.

"Is that a fish?" demanded Laddie. "It must be a whale."

"Oh!" shrieked Rose. "It's Russ! He'll be drowned!"

"Don't let him get wet, Rose," cried Margy. "Mother won't want him to get his clothes wet."

But if there was any part of Russ Bunker that was not wet when he managed to get on his feet and his head and shoulders appeared above the water, Rose couldn't imagine what part it could be. He was just the wettest boy she had ever seen.

Russ had got a footing finally upon the stone beside which the big catfish had lain. The water was too deep all around him for him to wade out. The bottom of the pool was so deep that it was over the boy's head. He had to stand on the rock and gasp for breath for he had swallowed a good deal of water, having gone down with his mouth open.

"What did I tell you?" demanded Frane, Junior, from the bank. "You couldn't catch that cat."

"I know it!" jerked out Russ. "I know it now."

"Lawsy me!" ejaculated Mammy June. "Is that the way you ketches catfish up Norf?"

The other little Bunkers did not understand this. Vi wanted to know at once if Russ had a kitty in the water with him. But nobody paid any attention to her questions.

"Here, you 'Lias and Henery!" commanded Mammy June to two of the older colored boys. "What you standin' there idle for? Go out on that bridge and haul that poor chile ashore. What a state he is in, to be sure!"

It did not take long to help Russ up on to the log again. The water just poured off him; but it was not very cold and his teeth didn't chatter - much. Mammy June showed anxiety, however.

"You come right into de house, honey," she said to Russ. "Now, little Miss," she added to Rose, "yo' mustn't scold him now. Wait till we wring his clothes out and get him dry. Yo' 'Lias, bring some dry bresh and some good sticks. We'll want a hot fire."

Mammy June had no stove in her cabin, but a broad and smoke-blackened open fireplace. There was a small fire in it, over which her teakettle hung. In five minutes the negro boys made a roaring blaze. Then the old woman drove them all out of the cabin save Russ, whom she helped off with his wet clothes, rubbed dry with a big towel, and to whom she gave a shirt and trousers to put on while she wrung out his clothing and hung it all about the fire to dry.

"That shirt and them pants," she said, "b'longs to my Sneezer - my Ebenezer. If he was here this wouldn't have happened to yo', honey. He wouldn't have let no w'ite boy fall into that branch - no, sir. But these no-'count other young ones didn't know 'nough to tell yo' that that ain't the way to catch catfish."

"I found out myself," admitted Russ rather ruefully.

Rose came to the door and begged to know if Russ was all right.

"He's going to be just as soon as I get him made a hot drink," declared Mammy June.

"Has he got all over being drowned?" Margy demanded.

And even Mun Bun was a good deal troubled because Russ had got so wet. "If you had any candy in your pocket, Russ," the little boy said, "it must be all soft now. It won't be good to eat."

"I didn't have any candy, Mun Bun," Russ told him. Russ was feeling a whole lot better now. Mammy June gave him a nice hot, sweet drink. He didn't mind if it was a little "stingy" too.

"Yo' all come in yere - yo' little w'ite folks," said Mammy June, "and we'll make some 'lasses taffy. I got plenty sorgum 'lasses. We can make it w'ile this catfish boy is getting dry."

She continued to call Russ "the catfish boy" and chuckled over his adventure. But she warned him, when his clothing was dry, that he must be more careful when he was playing about the water.

"An' yo' got to tell yo' mudder and daddy about it," she instructed Russ. "Don't never hide nothin' from 'em."

"Oh, we don't!" Rose broke in. "We always tell Mother and Daddy everything."

"That's what I tell my Philly and Ally and Frane, Junior. Always must tell they parents."

"And get scolded for it," said Phillis rather crossly.

"Well, then," said Mammy June cheerfully, "you mustn't do things to get scolded for. So I tell all these grandchildren of mine. Scat, you children!" for she saw several of the smaller colored boys and girls trying to steal in at the cabin door. "Ain't room for you in here noways. Yo' shall have yo' share of the 'lasses candy when it's done."

That "taffy pull" was a famous one. The six little Bunkers

thought they had never eaten such nice molasses candy as Mammy June made. Phillis Armatage made believe that she did a lot to help for she buttered the pans. But it was Mammy June who really did it all.

"I think," confessed Rose to Alice, "that it is awfully nice to have both a mammy and a mother, as you girls have. Of course, a mammy can't be just what Mother Bunker is to us; but Mammy June is nice."

"She's lots better to us than our mother, in some ways," said Alice bluntly. "Mother doesn't want us to play noisy in the house. She has headaches and stays on the couch a lot. We have to step soft and can't talk loud. But Mammy June never has the fidgets."

"What's 'fidgets'?" asked Rose, quite shocked by the way Alice spoke of her mother.

"What ladies have," explained Alice. "Don't your mother have 'em?"

"I guess not. I never heard about them," Rose answered. "Then if your mother is sick, I don't suppose she can help it. It is lucky you have got a mammy."

That first afternoon ("evening" all these Southern folks called it) at Mammy June's was a very pleasant experience. Russ did not mind his ducking - much. He only grinned a little when Mammy June called him "the catfish boy."

"Serves me good and right," he confessed to Rose. "I ought not to have gone into that brook without a bathing suit. And, anyway, I guess a boy can't catch fish of any kind with his hands."

Mun Bun and Margy and the smaller colored children managed to spread the molasses taffy over face and hands to a greater or less degree; but they enjoyed the taffy pull as much as the older children did. Finally, after Mammy June had washed his face and hands, Mun Bun climbed up into her comfortable lap and went fast asleep.

The old woman, who loved children so dearly and was so kind to them, looked at one of her older grandsons, Elias, and ordered him to "get de boxwagon to take dis bressed baby home in."

A soapbox on a plank between two pairs of wheels being produced and the box made comfortable with a quilt and a pillow belonging to Mammy June, Mun Bun was laid, still fast asleep, in this vehicle, and Russ started to drag his little brother home.

"Yo' 'Lias!" exclaimed Mammy June, from the doorway of her cabin, "whar's yo' manners? Don't you let that w'ite visitor boy drag that boxwagon. You get busy, 'Lias."

Russ and the other Bunker children were not used to being waited on at every step and turn. But they became better used to it as the time passed. The white folks on the Meiggs Plantation seemed to expect all this aid from the colored folks, and the latter seemed willing and eager to attend.

Russ was not scolded for his involuntary plunge into the branch. In fact his father laughed immensely at the tale. But Mother Bunker had to be assured that the stream was neither deep nor boisterous before she could laugh much.

The children had all had a lovely afternoon at Mammy June's and after that day they found most of their enjoyment in running down to her cabin and playing there. This delight was shared by the Armatages too. And the latter's father and mother seemed perfectly content if the children were in mammy's care.

The days passed all too swiftly. Everybody, darkies and all, were on tiptoe about the coming festival of Christmas and

New Year's. The six little Bunkers learned that these holidays were celebrated in different style on this Georgia plantation from what they were in the North.

CHAPTER XV

WHEN CHRISTMAS IS FOURTH OF JULY

Mun Bun and Margy were too little always to accompany the older children on their rambles; but the two smallest Bunkers could be trusted to invent plays of their own when they might be left out of the older one's parties. They had long since learned not to feel slighted if Mother Bunker decided that they were to stay near her.

There was sufficient mystery and expectation regarding the coming holiday celebrations at the Meiggs Plantation to excite the little folks in any case. There was to be no Christmas tree such as the Bunkers had had the previous Christmas in the North. Both Mun Bun and Margy could remember that tree very clearly.

But there was quite as much hiding of funny shaped packages until the gift day should arrive, and the house was being decorated, inside and out, for the coming celebration. Mun Bun and Margy watched the servants hanging Christmas greens and mistletoe, although, unlike the older little Bunkers, they could not go into the swamps with the men to gather these greens.

"We just ought to have a Christmas tree of our own," Margy said to Mun Bun. "I know where we can get a tree, and we'll beg some wreaths and trimming from that nice colored man there."

"We can't," said Mun Bun, somewhat despondently. "We isn't got a house to put the tree in. And we had the Christmas tree last time in the house."

"I've found a house," whispered Margy. "But don't you tell anybody."

"Not even tell Muvver?" asked Mun Bun, looking almost scared. Yet the idea of a secret delighted him too.

"Not till we get it all done. Then we will show her how fine it is," said Margy.

"Where is your house?" asked Mun Bun.

"You come along and I'll show you. I found it all by myself."

She led Mun Bun by the hand out behind the big house and toward the quarters. In a sheltered place, behind a hedge, was a little house, sure enough. And it was not so very little after all, for when they went into it they could both stand upright.

"There isn't any window," said Mun Bun. "This isn't a regular house."

"Of course, it's a house," Margy declared. "It's got a doorway, and -"

"It hasn't got any door, just the same," said Mun Bun, who might have liked the house better if he had found it himself.

"We don't need a door. We want it open so the big folks can see our tree when we get it trimmed."

"Where is the tree?" demanded the still doubtful little boy.

"Now, Mun Bun!" exclaimed Margy, "do you want to play at fixing this Christmas tree, or don't you?"

"Oh, yes," said Mun Bun, who did not really want to be left out of any fun, even if he did not think of it first himself. "Show me the tree, Margy."

"Of course I will," said his sister. "You must help me get it and carry it in here."

"Come on," urged the little boy. "Let's."

So then Margy showed him where the tree she had found stood in a green tub outside the door of a small house that was almost all glass. The lower panes of glass in this house were whitewashed, so the children could not see what was in it; but this tree with its thick, glossy leaves seemed to have been left out for anybody to take who wanted it.

They had to tug pretty hard to get the tree out of the tub. As Margy said, they didn't want the tub anyway, for it would take up too much room. And they were not strong enough to move it.

But they got the tree uprooted, and then were able to carry it to the little house that Margy had selected as their own private dwelling for the play celebration.

By dragging the tree inside, roots first, they managed to get it in without breaking off any of the glossy leaves. They stood it upright and made it steady by placing some bricks that they found about the roots. Its top reached the roof of the little house.

They begged some broken wreaths and chains of evergreen and even a spray of mistletoe with berries on it. The workmen were very kind to the smallest Bunkers. Mun Bun grew quite as excited and enthusiastic as Margy. They worked hard to trim that tree.

"But it hasn't any lights," said Mun Bun sadly. "And that other Christmas tree had lights."

You see, he remembered very clearly about that. And when Mun Bun played he always wanted the play to be as real as possible.

"We'll get candles," declared Margy. "I saw candles in the kitchen house where that nice cook lives. Let's go and ask her."

But just as they were going to squeeze out of the low door of the little house they heard a great shouting and calling, and then suddenly the snapping of explosive crackers - fire crackers - began!

"Oh!" gasped Mun Bun. "Who's shootin'?"

"It's firecrackers. You know, we've had 'em before. And they are in a barrel," said Margy breathlessly.

Through the doorway of the little house in which they had set up the "Christmas tree" the two saw their brothers and sisters, the Armatage children, and a lot of the little negroes dancing about a barrel a little way down the hill. Margy was right. Into that barrel somebody had thrown a lighted bunch of firecrackers - about the safest way in which those noisy and delightful "snappers" can be exploded.

And what a noise they made! Mun Bun and Margy almost forgot their own play for the moment as they struggled to see which should first go out of the door of the little house. Getting in each other's way, they were delayed and before they could get out a great dog came bounding toward them.

"Oh! Oh! Oh!" squealed Margy, and shrank back, leaving to Mun Bun the opportunity of getting out if he wanted to.

"I'm not afraid of that dog," said Mun Bun. But, just the same, he did not go out when he might have done so. "He isn't as big as Aunt Jo's Alexis, is he, Margy?"

"But we aren't acquainted with him like we were with Alexis," whispered the little girl.

She knew his name was Bobo. But always before when she had seen him the great hound, with his flappy ears and wide mouth, had been chained.

"Do - do you suppose he'll want to bite us?" quavered Mun Bun, admitting now that he was afraid of the dog. "And what does he want here in our house, Margy?"

Margy suddenly remembered that when she had seen Bobo before he had been chained right at this little house. Maybe it was his house, although it was bigger than any doghouse she had ever seen before.

"We don't want him in here," cried Mun Bun. "There isn't any room for him." Then he cried to the big hound: "Go 'way! You'll spoil our Christmas tree."

The big hound came nearer, but more quietly. His eyes were red, and he sniffed enquiringly at the doorway while the children crowded back against the tree. Perhaps he was the very kindest dog in the world; but to Mun Bun and Margy he appeared to be dreadfully savage!

"Go 'way!" they shouted in chorus. And Mun Bun added again: "We don't want him in here, do we, Margy?"

The dog seemed determined to thrust himself into the house. Perhaps Bobo felt about Mun Bun and Margy as they did about him - that they had no right there, and he wanted them to get out. And when he put his great head and shoulders into the doorway the little Bunkers began to shriek at the top of their voices.

Even the snapping firecrackers could not drown their voices now. Russ and Rose heard the cries coming from the doghouse, and they knew Mun Bun and Margy were in trouble. They saw Bobo, who had been with them to the swamp, seemingly stuck half way in the doorway of his kennel, and Russ cried:

"I guess that's where they are. Hear 'em, Rose? Come on, save Mun Bun and Margy."

"I'm afraid of that hound," replied Rose, but she followed her brother just the same.

Russ shouted to the dog. The hound backed out and looked around at Russ Bunker. But his red eyes did not scare the boy.

"We're coming, Mun Bun!" Russ shouted. "We're coming, Margy!"

The two little ones appeared at the door of the kennel. They were not crying much, but they had tight hold of each other's hands.

"Russ! Rose!" cried Margy. "Take us out."

"What are you doing in that dog's kennel?" demanded Rose.

"Playing Christmas," said Margy, with quivering voice.

"I guess it isn't Christmas," said Mun Bun doubtfully. "I guess it's Fourth of July. Isn't it, Russ? They don't have shooters only on the Fourth of July."

"They do down here," said Russ, reaching the kennel and looking in while Bobo stood by as though he still wondered why Mun Bun and Margy had tried to turn him out of his house.

Just then one of the colored men, who was a gardener, came along and stooped to look into the kennel too.

"For de lan's sake!" he cried, "what you childern doin' in dat dog kennel?"

"We - we were playing Christmas tree," said Margy, grabbing hold of Rose's hand.

"For de lan's sake!" repeated the man, showing the whites of his eyes in a most astonishing way. "What dat in dere?"

"That's our Christmas tree," said Mun Bun, very bravely now.

"For de lan's sake!" ejaculated the man for a third time. "What Mistah Armatage gwine to say now? Dat's his bestest rubber plant what he tol' me to take partic'lar care of. What will you lil' w'ite childern be up to next, I'm a-wondering?"

CHAPTER XVI

A LETTER AND A BIG LIGHT

"Why, Mun Bun!" murmured Russ.

"Why, Margy Bunker!" exclaimed Rose.

Mun Bun was staring with all his eyes (and he had two very bright ones) at the rubber plant. He did not consider the mischief he had done. He was as curious as Vi could possibly have been about an entirely different thing.

"If that's a rubber plant, Russ," he demanded, "where's the rubbers? I don't see any overshoes on it. What part of it is rubber?"

At that the black man threw back his head and laughed loudly. The children all watched his open mouth and rolling eyes and flashing teeth and finally they broke into laughter too. They could not help it.

"But," said Russ, after they had stopped laughing, "I am afraid Mr. Armatage will be angry with us."

"I dunno - I dunno, chile," said the negro, shaking his head. "He sure is partic'lar 'bout dat rubber plant. But mebbe I can repot it and fix it up all right. It's only just been uprooted, and I was gwine to change de dirt in dat tub, anyway."

"Oh! Do you think you can do it and save Mun Bun and Margy from getting a scolding?" Rose cried.

"We'll see, lil' Miss. Shouldn't wonder," and the gardener went to work at once.

Meanwhile Bobo sat on his haunches and mournfully looked at what was going on. His red eyes had a very sad expression and his drooping ears made him look, so Rose said, more mournful still.

"He looks as if he'd just come from a funeral," she said to Russ.

"What's that?" demanded Margy promptly.

But Rose and Russ dodged that question. In fact they did not know how to explain just what a funeral was. But in watching the gardener replace the rubber plant in the green tub, surrounded with fresh earth from the green house, the little ones forgot everything else, even Bobo.

Bobo, just as soon as he could, went into his house and smelled all around and finally lay down, his muzzle sticking out of the door.

"He looks unhappy," Rose said. "I guess he thought he wasn't going to have any home at all when he saw you two in there with the rubber plant."

"It was a good Christmas tree," was Margy's only reply to this.

"But we didn't get the candles to light it up," Mun Bun rejoined, walking away hand in hand with Russ. "So how could it be a Christmas tree if there weren't any candles?"

As Christmas Day grew closer there was less work done and more play engaged in by everybody on the plantation. Christmas Eve there was a beautiful display of fireworks on the front lawn of the big house, and everybody from the quarters came to see it, as well as the white folks. Even Mammy June came up from her cabin by the stream, walking with difficulty, for she was lame, and sat in state on the porch "with de w'ite folks" to see the fireworks.

The old woman had taken a strong liking to the six little Bunkers and she made as much of them as she did of the three little Armatages. But the latter were not jealous at all. Phillis and Alice and Frane, Junior, were likewise delighted with the children from the North.

Christmas Day dawned brilliantly, and although there was what Mr. Armatage called "a tang" in the air it was so warm that it was hard for the Bunker children to realize that this was the day that they expected up North to be "white."

"A 'white Christmas' doesn't mean anything down here in Georgia," said Daddy Bunker. "Though once in a while they have a little snow here. But they never speak of it - not the natives. It is a sort of scandal in the family," and he laughed, looking at Mother Bunker, who understood him if the children did not.

But white or green, that Christmas Day was a delightful one. Even without a gaudily lighted and trimmed tree, the Bunkers were pleased in every way. Their presents were stacked with those belonging to the Armatage children under the chimney-piece in the big front parlor, and Mr. Armatage himself made the presentations.

There were presents from "all over" for the six little Bunkers; for no matter how far they were away from their many relatives and friends, the six were fondly remembered. Even Cowboy Jack sent gifts from Texas!

With the presents from Aunt Jo came a letter particularly addressed to the children. Russ read it aloud to them all. It gave news of William's neuralgia (Vi still insisted on calling it "croup") and about Annie and Parker. Even the Great Dane, Alexis, was mentioned. But the most important thing spoken of in the letter to the children's minds was the fact that Aunt Jo said she meant to keep Sam, the colored boy Mun Bun and Margy had introduced into her Back Bay home, all winter.

"The boy is really a treasure," said Aunt Jo. "He can do something besides dance - although he does plenty of that in the kitchen to the delight of Parker, Annie and William. He has been taught to work, and is really a very good houseboy. And he looks well in his uniform."

"I'd like to see him in a uniform," said Laddie. "Is he a soldier, or a policeman?"

"He's a 'buttons,'" replied Mother Bunker, laughing. "Aunt Jo has always wanted to have a boy in buttons to answer the door and clean the knives."

"I'd rather see him dance again," said Russ, and he slyly tried to cut that pigeon wing once more. But he made a dismal failure of it.

There was dancing in plenty at the negro quarters that Christmas evening. All the white folks went down from the big house to watch the proceedings. And again Mammy June was there.

There had been a great feast for the hands, but although one grinning negro boy confessed to Russ that he was "full o' tuck," he still could dance. This boy was applauded vigorously by his mates, and one of them called out:

"'Lias! show dese w'ite folks how *to* cut dat pigeon wing. Go on, boy!"

"Lawsy me!" exclaimed Mammy June, "don't none of you know how to do dat like my Sneezer. If he was here he'd show 'em. Just you dance plain, honey. Double shuffle's as much as you can do."

So her grandson, 'Lias, did not try any fancy steps. Privately, however, and much to Rose's amusement, Russ Bunker often tried to copy Sam's pigeon-wing step.

"If we ever go to Aunt Jo's again - and of course we shall - I am going to get Sam to show me how to do it. I'll get it perfect some time," sighed the oldest Bunker boy.

Vi, looking on at one of her brother's attempts, asked:

"Doesn't it hurt the pigeon to cut its wing?"

But that was a silly question, and they all laughed at her. Laddie grew suddenly excited.

"Oh! I know a new riddle!" he cried. "It's a good riddle!"

"What is it?" asked his twin sister.

"It isn't a good riddle just because you made it up, Laddie," said Rose.

"It would be a good one no matter who made it up," answered Laddie decidedly. "You let me tell it. I know it's good."

"What is it, Laddie?" Russ Bunker asked.

"Here is the riddle," said Laddie eagerly. "What sort of wing has no feathers on it? And the answer is, of course, 'A pigeon wing.' There! Isn't that a fine riddle?"

"Pooh!" said Vi. "I don't think so."

"Some pigeons' wings have feathers," said Rose.

"Hoh!" cried Laddie, somewhat disturbed. "That one Russ was trying to make doesn't have any feathers on it."

"That's only one kind, and it isn't really a pigeon's wing, you know."

Laddie stared at his sister, Rose, with much doubt. "You're always disappointing me, Rose," he murmured.

"But Rose is right, Laddie," said Russ. "And there are other wings that have no feathers."

"What wings?" grumbled Laddie.

"I know!" cried Vi suddenly. "Airplane wings! They haven't any feathers."

"But they are no more like real wings," complained Rose, "than Russ's dancing step."

"No," said the oldest Bunker boy. "I mean bat's wings. Don't you remember that bat we caught that time? Its wings didn't have feathers at all. It was covered with fur."

"Oh, well," sighed Laddie. "Then my riddle isn't any good."

"Not much, I am afraid," said Russ kindly but firmly.

However, Laddie and the other little Bunkers did not have many disappointing things happen to them on this lovely Christmas Day. Mr. and Mrs. Armatage tried in every way to make the stay of their guests at the Meiggs Plantation as pleasant as possible.

After the celebration at the quarters the white folks came home, and there at the big house a fine party was soon under way. People had come in their cars from far and near and the house was brilliantly lighted on the first two floors.

The children were allowed to look on at this grown folks' party for a little while, then they had to go to bed. Phillis and Alice and Frane, Junior, seemed to consider it very hard that they were not allowed to stay downstairs; but the little Bunkers were used to having their own good times and did not expect to enter into the amusements of their elders.

"Let's sit on the top step of these stairs," said Phillis to Rose and Alice, "and we can see through the balustrades. There's Mrs. Campron! She's got a lovely dress on, and diamonds."

Rose remained with the two Armatage girls for a little while and Russ saw to it that the little folks went to bed. Then he came out into the hall again to see what the girls were doing. Before he could ask them he chanced to look out of the back window at the end of the long hall.

"Oh!" cried Russ Bunker. "What is that?"

"What's what?" demanded Phillis. "What do you see?"

"Is it a shooting star?" went on Russ. "See that light! I believe it must be a fire."

The girls came running to join him then, more interested in what Russ saw than they were in what was going on at the party below.

CHAPTER XVII

MAMMY JUNE IN PERIL

From the big house on the Meiggs Plantation, standing on a knoll - which means a small hill, - one could see for a long distance all about, in spite of the shade trees, and especially when looking from the third floor windows. Russ Bunker was looking right out over the quarters where the hands lived, and could see far down the slope of the land and to the forest beyond the cultivated fields.

It was a lovely starlit night, but of course the stars did not reveal everything. The strong red light that sprang up beyond the cabins where the colored people lived, revealed a great deal, however.

"It's a house afire!" declared Phillis Armatage.

"Where can there be a house in that direction?" Rose Bunker asked. "Isn't that fire beyond the cabins, Russ?"

Russ suddenly sprang to action. He wheeled from the window and ran along the hall to the stairway.

"Russ! Russ! Where are you going?" demanded his sister.

"Tell Daddy and Mr. Armatage. I know what house is afire. It's Mammy June's cabin!" shouted Russ.

He had previously located the direction of the old woman's cabin by the stream, and Russ was sure that he was right now. He left the girls screaming after him; he had no time to tell them how he was so sure of his statement.

Down the two flights of stairs he plunged until he landed with a bang on the hall rug at the foot of the lower flight. He almost fell against Mr. Armatage himself when he landed. And Daddy Bunker was not far away.

"Well, well, young man, what's this?" demanded Mr. Armatage, for a moment quite as stern with Russ as he was with his own children.

Daddy, too, looked upon Russ with amazement. "Why, Russ," he said, "what does this mean? What are you doing down here?"

"There's a fire!" gasped out Russ, his breath almost gone. "There's a fire!"

"Upstairs?" demanded Mr. Armatage, whirling toward the stairway.

"Oh, no, sir! No, sir!" cried Russ, stopping him. "It's down the hill. I saw it from the window."

"The quarters?" demanded the planter.

"No, sir. It looks like Mammy June's. It's a great red flame shooting right up about where her cabin is."

"And the old woman has gone home. She's lame. Like enough she won't get out in time - if it is her shack. Come on, boys!" The planter's shout rang through the lower rooms and startled both the guests and the servants. "There's a fire down by the branch. May be a cabin and somebody in it. Come on in your cars and follow me. Get all the buckets you can find."

He dashed out of the house, hatless as he was, shouting to the colored folks who were gathered outside watching the dancing through the long windows. Daddy Bunker followed right behind him. And what do you suppose Russ did? Why, he could have touched Daddy Bunker's coat-tails he kept so close to him! Nobody forbade him, so Russ went too.

Mr. Armatage and Mr. Bunker got into one of the first cars to start, and Russ, with a water pail in each hand, got in too. There was a great noise of shouting and the starting of the motor-cars. Men ran hither and thither, and all the time the light of the fire down by the stream increased.

When they were under way, Mr. Armatage's car leading, they found many of the plantation hands running down the grassy road in advance. The cars passed these men, Mr. Armatage shouting orders as the car flew by. In two minutes they came to the clearing in which Mammy June's cabin stood. One end of the little house was all ablaze.

"The poor soul hasn't got out," cried Mr. Armatage, and with Mr. Bunker he charged for the door, burst it in, and dashed into the smoke which filled the interior.

Russ thought that Daddy Bunker was very brave indeed to do this. It looked to the boy as though both men would be burned by the raging fire. But he was brave himself. He fought back his tears and ran to the stream to fill with water both the pails he carried.

When he came staggering back with the filled pails, the water slopping over his shoes, the first of the hands arrived. One man grabbed Russ's pails and threw the water upon the burning logs. Such a small amount of water only made the flames hiss and the logs steam. But soon other filled pails were brought. More of the cars with guests from the party arrived, and a chain of men to the stream was formed.

Almost at once Mr. Armatage and Daddy Bunker fought their

way out of the burning cabin through the smoke, and they bore between them the screaming old woman. Mammy June was badly frightened.

"You're all right now, Mammy," declared Mr. Armatage, when he and Mr. Bunker put her into the tonneau of the car. "Here, boy!" he added to Russ, "you stay with her."

"I got to lose all! I got to lose ma home!" wailed Mammy June. "If my Ebenezer had been yere, dat chimbley wouldn't have cotched fire."

"Can't be helped now," said Daddy Bunker soothingly. "We'll try to save your home, Mammy."

But although their intentions were of the best, this could not be done. The cabin - as dry as a stack of straw - could not be saved. The pails were passed from hand to hand as rapidly as possible, but the fire had gained such headway that it was impossible to quench it until the cabin was in complete ruins.

"You be mighty glad, Mammy June," said Mr. Armatage, finally giving up the unequal battle, "that you are saved yourself. And you wouldn't have been if this little Bunker hadn't seen the fire when he did."

"Bless him!" groaned the old woman, hugging Russ to her side in the car. "If my Ebenezer had been home it wouldn't never have happened, Mistah Armatage."

She harped upon this belief incessantly as they finally drove back to the big house. The fright and exposure quite turned Mammy June's brain for the time. She was somewhat delirious.

"S'pose my Ebenezer come home and find de cabin in ruins. He mebbe will think Mammy June burned up, and go right off again. And he might come any time!"

The old woman talked of this even after they put her to bed and a doctor who chanced to be at Mrs. Armatage's party had attended her. The fire, and her bodily illness, had prostrated the old woman.

The end of that Christmas party was not as pleasant as the beginning. It was long after midnight before even the children were in their beds and composed for sleep. The party broke up at an earlier hour than might have been expected.

Rose slept in the room with Phillis and Alice Armatage. Just as she was dropping to sleep and after her companions were already in dreamland Rose saw the door of the room pushed open. The moon had risen, and Rose recognized Russ's tousled head poked in the open door.

"What do you want?" she demanded in a whisper. "Oh, Russ! there isn't another fire, is there?"

"No! Hush! I just thought of something."

"What is it?" asked Rose in the same low tone that Russ used.

"We can do something for Mammy June."

"We can't cure her rheumatism, Russ," said Rose. "Even the doctor can't do that in a hurry. He said so."

"No. She's worrying about her boy. That boy with the funny name. Sneezer."

"Yes, I know," said Rose.

"She is afraid he will come back and find the cabin burned and go away again without her knowing it," said Russ gravely, tiptoeing to his sister's bedside.

"Yes. Mother says it's real pitiful the way she takes on," sighed the little girl.

"Well, Rose, you and I can help about that," said Russ confidently.

"How can we?" she asked, in surprise.

"We can write a sign and stick it up on a pole down there by the burned cabin. We'll make a sign saying that Mammy June is up here at the big house and for Sneezer to come and see her."

"Oh, goody!" cried Rose, but still under her breath. "That's a fine idea, Russ."

"Don't say anything about it to anybody," warned her brother, eager to make a secret of the plan that had popped into his head. "We'll write that sign early in the morning and go down there and stick it up. Want to?"

"Of course I do," said Rose, with a glad little jump in her bed. "I think you're just the smartest boy, Russ, to think of it. I won't say a word about it, not even to Philly and Alice."

With this plan dancing in her head Rose soon fell asleep while Russ stole back to the room where he slept with the smaller boys. After that the big house on the Meiggs Plantation became quiet for the rest of the long night.

CHAPTER XVIII

THE TWINS IN TROUBLE

Laddie and Vi Bunker felt as though they had been cheated. They had not been allowed to go to the fire, "when Mammy June's cabin had been burned all up," Vi declared. They had only seen the fire from an upper window of the big Armatage house.

"But it wasn't burned *up*, Vi," her twin insisted. "It was burned *down*."

"Russ said it was burned up when he came back from the fire - so now," Violet declared somewhat warmly.

"How can a house burn up? It just fell all to pieces into the cellar."

"There wasn't any cellar to Mammy June's house," Vi observed.

"Well, it fell down; so of course, it burned down."

"The flames went up," repeated Vi, quite as determinedly. "And the wood went with 'em - with the flames and smoke. So the cabin burned up."

What might have been the result of this discussion it would be hard to say had not the twins both felt so keenly their disappointment. Russ had gone to the fire and brought Mammy June out of the cabin and brought her up here to the big house! To tell the truth, Russ was so excited when he got back that in telling of the adventure he gave the younger children to understand that he had done it all himself. Daddy Bunker and Mr. Armatage did not appear much in his story.

"Russ is always doing the big things," sighed Laddie. "It's just like a riddle -"

"What is?" almost snapped Vi, for she was just as disappointed as her twin brother.

"Why, Russ getting the best of everything. Why is it?" muttered Laddie, kicking a pebble before him in the path.

"If that's a riddle, I can't answer it," said Vi.

"It isn't any worse to ask riddles than it is to ask questions - so now."

The twins were not always in accord, of course; but they were seldom so near to a quarrel as upon this morning. Perhaps, for one thing, the day before, they had rather over-done and possibly had over-eaten. They were on the verge of doing something that the Bunker children seldom did - quarreling. Fortunately something suddenly attracted Laddie's attention and he stopped kicking the pebble and pointed down the yard in front of them.

"Oh, Vi! See that cunning thing! What is it?"

Something flashed across a green patch of grass away down by the road. It was red, had small, sharp-pointed ears and nose and a bushy tail. This tail waved quite importantly as the small animal ran.

"Come on!" cried Vi, taking the lead at once. She often did so, for Laddie was slower than she. "Come on! Let's get it, Laddie."

Laddie, nothing loath, ran after his twin sister. They raced down the hill and came to the little gully into which the animal with the bushy tail had disappeared. The end of that gully was the open mouth of a culvert under the road.

"Did he go in there?" Laddie demanded. "Did he go into that hole, Vi?"

"He must have," declared Violet. "It must be his home. It's a burrow."

"But he wasn't a bunny. Bunnies have burrows," objected Laddie.

"I guess other animals can have burrows, too," said his twin. "And he was lots prettier than a rabbit."

"He was that," admitted the excited Laddie. "It wasn't a rabbit, of course. Rabbits aren't red."

"Let's find the other end of the hole," Vi said eagerly. "We'll stop both ends up and then - and then -"

"Well, what then?" her twin demanded.

"Why, we can catch him then," said Vi, rather feebly. "That is, we can if he wants to come out."

"I suppose we can. If he doesn't take too long. Let's," said Laddie, and he ran across the road and looked to see if there was another opening to the culvert.

But as it chanced, this was an old and unused drain, and the farther mouth of it was stopped up. This made the hole a very nice den for the little animal the Bunker twins had seen go into it. But neither Laddie nor Vi had any idea as to what the creature was.

"I'm going to get a stick and poke him out," announced Laddie.

"You can't poke him out when there is no other hole over there," rejoined Vi very sensibly.

"I'll poke him till he comes out then," said Laddie, looking all about but not starting to find a stick.

To tell the truth he was at the end of his resources. He did not know how to get at the little red animal.

"Anyway," he said at last, "maybe he didn't run in here after all."

"He did so, Laddie Bunker!" cried Violet. "I saw him."

This seemed final. Laddie looked all around again, quite puzzled as to what to do next. There was no backing out of a thing when once it was begun - not with Vi Bunker! She always insisted upon going on to the end, no matter what that end might be.

"Well," her twin said at last, "I s'pose I'll have to go in after him."

"How can you?" asked Vi promptly, but excitedly, too.

"I can crawl into that hole -"

"Isn't it too small?"

"Well, I'm not so big," replied Laddie. "I guess I can do it. I'm going to try."

He knelt down before the round mouth of the culvert. It was a piece of drainpipe with a rough rim at the edge of the hole. Laddie poked his head into the hole.

"It's as dark as the inside of your pocket, Vi Bunker," he said, in a muffled voice.

"Shall I run get a candle?" asked his sister.

"No," sighed Laddie; and even his sigh sounded funny from inside the pipe. "If you do they'll want to know what you want it for. And if we are going to catch this - this whatever-it-is, we want to catch it all by ourselves. Wait."

Vi granted that request. She waited, watching Laddie's plump little body wriggling farther and farther into the culvert. His jacket caught several times on the rough rim of the opening. But he persevered.

"Oh!" ejaculated Laddie at last, and his voice seemed a murmur from a great way off.

"I guess you better come back, Laddie," said Vi, getting anxious.

Laddie, if the truth were known, thought so too. For just then he had sighted in the dark two fiery points, like flashing bits of glass or mica. He knew what they were; they were the eyes of the little red animal he had chased into this hole. And Laddie thought that when eyes flashed so brilliantly, their owner must be angry.

"He's going to jump at me!" breathed the little boy to himself.

He began to back out hastily. The bottom of his jacket caught on the rim of the pipe. He was stuck there!

"Pull! Pull me out, Vi Bunker!" he shouted.

But his voice was so muffled that his sister could not understand what he said. It looked as though Laddie was unable to get back the way he had come. And he certainly dared not go on ahead.

For now, to increase his fears, he saw other points of light in the darkness - all in pairs, the eyes of several smaller animals, he was sure! He had self-control enough to count them and found that there were five pairs of eyes altogether.

What should he do about it? Struggle as he might he could not back any farther. And no manner of wriggling was likely to get him out of the hole the way he had come in.

CHAPTER XIX

IN MAMMY JUNE'S ROOM

Russ and Rose had both got up very early the day after Christmas, for their minds were filled with the idea of helping Mammy June. The poor old woman's anxiety should be relieved, and the two oldest of the Bunker children were determined that they would relieve it regarding her son, "Sneezer," if that were possible.

So Russ found some cardboard boxes that had held certain of their Christmas presents, and he tore these apart and they wrote carefully a message to the old woman's absent son on both faces of these cards. At least, Russ wrote them, for by now he had learned at school to write a very good hand. Rose was not so sure - especially about her "q's" and capital "S's." Anybody who could read handwriting at all, however, could have read those signs that Russ Bunker wrote.

"It doesn't seem like Christmas time at all," Rose said, as the two ran down the lane right after breakfast toward the branch and the burned cabin. "See the leaves and grass! And there's a flower!"

It was only a weed, but it was a pretty one and Rose gathered it - of course for Mother Bunker. When they came in sight of Mammy June's cabin it was a sad looking place indeed. The little Bunkers had had several nice visits to the old woman's cabin, and they were really very sorry that it had burned down.

The disaster was complete. The log walls were tumbled in heaps and were all charred. The interior of the hut was little but ashes.

"Oh!" cried Rose. "If that Sneezer Meiggs did come home and see all this, he might go away again, just as his mother says. It would be too dreadful, Russ. I am so glad you invented this idea of putting up signs for him."

In fact, Russ was quite proud of his original thought himself. He was naturally of an inventive turn of mind and this was not the first novel thought he had expressed. He and Rose stuck up the cards on poles that they found near by, and they had so many of them that they quite surrounded the ashes of the old hut.

"He can't help seeing them if he comes here," said Rose, as they departed from the spot. "But do you s'pose he'll ever want to come back to the place where everybody called him 'Sneezer'?"

"He ought to want to come back to see Mammy June," declared Russ warmly. "I think she is just fine."

"So do I," admitted Rose reflectively. "But I wouldn't want to be called by such a name as Sneezer."

It was when they got back to the big house and around to its front that the two oldest little Bunkers became aware that something was happening down by the road. They saw Vi hopping up and down in a funny fashion, and she was screaming.

"Now, what do you suppose is the matter with her?" demanded Rose.

"Don't know. But it's something, sure enough!" rejoined Russ, and he started on a run for the spot where Violet was jumping up and down and screaming.

As Russ and Rose started down the hill the three Armatage children came out of the front door of the big house and ran after them, screaming as well. Then appeared a host of small colored folk - Russ and Rose never could imagine where they all came from. They seemed to spring right up out of the ground when anything exciting happened.

All this troop came streaming down the hill, and very quickly Vi found herself surrounded. Russ demanded:

"What's the matter with you? Has something bitten you?"

"They are biting Laddie!" wailed the twin sister.

"How silly!" exclaimed Phillis Armatage. "Laddie isn't here."

"Yes, he is, so now!" cried Vi.

"Oh! Oh!" screamed Alice. "I see his legs!"

At that they all saw his legs - at least, as much of them as were poked out of the mouth of the drainpipe. And they certainly were kicking vigorously. But the children outside made so much noise that the voice of the boy inside the pipe could not be heard.

"Oh! Oh!" declared Vi, jumping up and down again. "It is biting him."

"What is biting him? Mosquitoes?" demanded Russ, as much puzzled as anybody.

"The red thing! With the pointed ears! And a big tail!" cried Vi in gasps.

"What can she mean?" demanded Rose.

But Philly Armatage suspected the reason for Vi's fear at once. She grabbed hold of Laddie's ankles and started to draw him out of the pipe.

"You'd better come out!" she cried. "That old fox will bite your nose off."

"A fox!" cried Russ, in wonder and alarm. "Does a fox live in that hole?"

"And she's got puppies. We saw 'em playing out here one day. Father is only waiting for a chance to smoke 'em out. They are terrible. They eat hens and other poultry."

Russ was vastly interested, as well as troubled by Laddie's fix. For the smaller boy was really wedged by his rolled-up jacket tight into the mouth of the culvert. His muffled cries became more imploring, and the other children really feared that the mother fox, fearing for her young, might have attacked the boy.

"I tell you he must be got out!" shouted Russ.

"How you going to do it?" Philly demanded. Then she called to Laddie: "Push in farther, Laddie! Then maybe you can back out all right."

But Laddie Bunker was so much afraid of the foxes by now (he still saw their luminous eyes before him) that he dared not squirm any deeper into the pipe. What would have happened to him finally - whether or not the old fox might not have attacked him - will never be known, for Russ Bunker took desperate means to release his brother.

Russ ran to a pile of cobblestones beside the road, seized a big one, and staggered back with it in both hands. With the stone he pounded the rim of the pipe so hard that it broke in pieces.

"Ow! Ow!" cried the muffled voice of Laddie Bunker. "You are breaking my legs. Don't pound me so!"

Laura Lee Hope

"Wriggle out! Hurry up! What's holding you?" demanded Russ, half angrily because he was so excited.

The smaller boy began to move backward now, the rough rim of the pipe no longer holding his jacket. Slowly he pushed out. When he appeared, his face very red and tear-streaked, Russ and Phillis pulled him to his feet.

"Where's the fox?" demanded Vi, still very much excited.

"Is that a fox?" demanded Laddie, panting.

"Yes," said Phillis Armatage.

"That fox has got five pairs of eyes, then," grumbled Laddie.

"She's got four pups," cried Frane, Junior. "I'm going to run and tell father," and he ran away up the hill.

"Come on!" cried Russ, immediately in action again. "Let's stop up the hole. Then the foxes can't get out until Mr. Armatage comes."

They did that - at least, Russ and Vi and the colored boys did. Rose dusted Laddie off and wiped his face. He soon became more cheerful.

"Well," he said, with a long breath, "they didn't bite me after all; but I thought they would. And their eyes shone dreadfully."

"What made them shine?" demanded Vi, her usual curiosity aroused.

"Because they were mad," said her twin promptly. "That old mother fox didn't want me in there."

The adventure was happily ended; that is, for Laddie and Vi. Not so for the foxes. For Mr. Armatage and the gardener came with shovel and club and they dug down to the foxes' den. But the children had not done their work of closing the entrance well, and just as Mr. Armatage broke through into her den, Mrs. Fox and her puppies scurried out and away into the pine woods. But she had to look for a new home, for her old one was completely broken up.

After this the little Bunkers and the Armatage children trooped up to the house and went to the room where Mammy June had been put to bed. The doctor had already been to see her this morning.

The old colored woman was propped up with pillows and she wore the usual turban on her head. She smiled delightedly when she saw the white children and hailed them as gayly as though she were not in pain.

"Lawsy me, childern!" cried Mammy June. "Has you come to see how I is? I sure has got good friends, I sure has! An' if Ebenezer Caliper Spotiswood Meiggs was back home yere where he b'longs, there wouldn't be a happier ol' woman in all Georgia - no, sir!

"For Mistah Armatage say he's gwine have me another house built before spring. And it'll be a lot mo' fixy than my ol' house - yes, sir! Wait till my Sneezer comes home and sees it - Tut, tut! He ain't mebbe comin' home no mo'!"

"Oh, yes, he will, Mammy June," Philly said comfortingly.

"Don't know. These boys ups and goes away from their mammies and ain't never seen nor heard of again."

"But Sneezer loved you too well to stay away always," Alice Armatage said.

"And when these Bunkers go back North," put in Frane, Junior, "they are going to look for Sneezer everywhere."

"You reckon you'll find him?" asked Mammy June of Rose.

"I hope so," said the oldest Bunker girl.

"Of course we will," agreed Russ stoutly. "And Daddy Bunker will look out for him too. He said so."

According to Russ's mind, that Daddy Bunker had promised to help find the lost boy seemed conclusive that Sneezer must be found. He and Rose began eagerly to tell Mammy June what they had already done to make it positive that Ebenezer Caliper Spotiswood Meiggs would not come back to the burned cabin some day and go away, thinking that his old mother was no longer alive.

"You blessed childern!" exclaimed Mammy June. "And has you fixed it dat way for me? But - but - you says you writ dem letters to Sneezer?"

"Yes," said Rose happily. "Yes, we did, Mammy June. And stuck them up on poles all about the burned house."

"I don't know! I don't know!" sighed the old woman. "I reckon dat won't be much use."

"Why not?" demanded Russ anxiously. "If he comes back he'll see and read 'em."

"No. No, sir! He may see 'em," said Mammy June, shaking her head on the pillow. "But he won't read 'em."

"Why won't he?" Russ demanded in some heat. "I wrote them just as plain as plain!"

"But," said Mammy June, still sadly, "you see, my Sneezer never learnt to read hand-writin'!"

CHAPTER XX

GOOSEY-GOOSEY-GANDER

The Bunker children, especially Russ and Rose, felt truly anxious because of Mammy June's unhappiness about her absent son. The boy they all called Sneezer should have been home now when his mother was crippled with rheumatism and had lost her home and all her little possessions.

She worried audibly and continually about Sneezer. Russ and Rose took counsel together more than once. They had hoped that their signs put up at the site of the burned cabin would have satisfied Mammy June that her son would come up to the big house whenever, or if ever, he returned to his old home. Now the Bunker children were not so sure.

When Russ and Rose told Philly Armatage what they had done she said:

"Mebbe he'll think the writing is just to keep ha'nts away. He can't read writing. He always worked in the fields or up here at the house. Those signs aren't any good - just as Mammy June says."

This opinion caused Russ and Rose additional anxiety. They did not know what to do about it. Even the boy's inventive mind was at fault in the emergency.

While the older Bunker brother and sister were troubled in this

Laura Lee Hope

way and Laddie and Vi were recovering from their adventure with the red fox, Margy and Mun Bun were, as usual, having their own pleasures and difficulties. The littlest Bunker was a born explorer. Daddy Bunker said so. And Margy was quite as active as the little fellow.

Hand in hand they wandered all about the big house and out-of-doors as well. There was always supposed to be somebody to watch them, especially if they went near the barns or paddocks where the horses and mules were. But sometimes the little folks slipped away from even Mother Bunker's observation.

The gardener often talked to the littlest Bunkers, and he saw, too, that they did no more mischief around the greenhouse. When he saw them that afternoon trotting down the hill toward the poultry houses he failed to follow them. He had his work to do, of course, and it did not enter his head that Mun Bun and Margy could get into much trouble with the poultry.

Margy and Mun Bun were delighted with the "chickens" as they called most of the fowl the Armatages kept. But there were many different kinds - not alone of hens and roosters; for there were peafowl, and guineas, and ducks, and turkeys. And in addition there was a flock of gray geese.

"Those are gooseys," Margy announced, pointing through the slats of the low fence which shut in the geese and their strip of the branch, or brook, and the grass plot which the geese had all to themselves.

"Goosey, goosey gander!" chanted Mun Bun, clinging to the top rail of the fence and looking through the slats. "Which is ganders and which is gooseys, Margy?"

As though in answer to his query one of the big birds, with a horny crown on its head, stuck out its neck and ran at the little boy looking through the fence. The bird hissed in a most hateful manner too.

"Oh, look out, Mun Bun!" cried his sister. "I guess that's a gander."

But Mun Bun, with a fence between him and the big bird, was as usual very brave.

"I don't have to look out, Margy Bunker," he declared proudly. "I am already out - so he can't get me. Anyway if he came after us I wouldn't let him bite you."

"I guess he would like to bite us," said the little girl, keeping well away from the fence herself.

"That's 'cause he must be hungry," said Mun Bun with confidence. "You see, he hasn't got anything but grass to eat. I guess they forgot to feed him and it makes him mad."

"That is too bad. He is a real pretty bird," agreed Margy. "Wonder if we could feed him?"

"We can ask that nice cook for bwead," said Mun Bun doubtfully.

"They don't feed gooseys bread, I guess," objected the little girl.

"What do they feed 'em?"

"I guess corn - or oats."

"Let's go and get some," said Mun Bun promptly, and he backed away from the fence, still keeping his gaze fixed on the threatening gander.

They both knew where the feed was kept, for they had watched the colored man feed the stock. So they went across to the stables. And nobody saw them enter the feed room.

As usual it did not trouble Margy and Mun Bun that they had

not asked permission to feed the geese. What they had not been literally forbidden to do the little folks considered all right. It was true that they were great ones for exploring and experimenting. That is how they managed to get into so much mischief.

In this matter, however, it did not seem as though Margy and Mun Bun could really get into much trouble. They got a little dish and filled it with corn and trotted back to the goose pen. This time the gander did not charge Mun Bun. But the whole flock was down the slope by the water and the little folks had to walk that way along the edge of the fenced lot.

They came to a place where a panel of the fence was crooked. It had been broken, in fact, and it was much easier to push it aside than not. Why! when Mun Bun leaned against it the strip of fence fell right over on to the grass of the goose yard.

"Now see what you've done, Mun Bun!" exclaimed Margy.

"Why - oh - I didn't mean to," sputtered Mun Bun.

"What do you s'pose Mr. Armatage will say?"

"He won't say anything," said Mun Bun briskly. "For he won't see it. And now, Margy, we can throw the corn to those gooseys and ganders much better. See!"

He grabbed a handful of shelled corn out of the dish and scattered it as far as he could toward the flock. At once the gray birds became interested. They stretched their long necks and the big gander uttered a questioning "honk!"

"It's corn - it's real corn!" cried Mun Bun. "Don't be afraid, goosey-goosey-gander," and he shouted with laughter.

Margy threw a handful of corn too. At once the geese drew nearer. When they reached the first kernels they began grabbing them up with that strange shoveling motion with their bills that all geese and ducks make. The children watched them with delight.

But as the geese waddled nearer the old gander began to wiggle his head from side to side and to hiss softly. Margy and Mun Bun looked at each other, and both drew back.

"I don't like that one much," said Margy. "Do you, Mun Bun?"

"I don't like him at all," confessed the little fellow. "I guess we'd better go back. Maybe Mother will be wanting us."

Margy turned as quickly as he did. She had not thrown out all the corn, but as she turned away a few kernels scattered from the dish. Instantly the gander saw this. With a long hiss he started after the two children, and many of his flock kept right behind their leader.

"Oh! Come quick, Mun Bun!" gasped Margy.

Mun Bun seized her hand. As they ran up the slope the corn scattered from the dish. This was enough to keep the flock following. But the big gander did not chase the little boy and girl because of the scattered corn. He was really angry!

The chubby legs of Mun Bun and Margy looked good to that old gander. He ran hissing after them and began to flap his wings. One stroke of one of those wings would knock down either of the children.

CHAPTER XXI

ROSE HAS AN IDEA

It was just like a nightmare, and both Margy and Mun Bun knew what nightmares were. Those are dreams that, when you are "sleeping them," you get chased by something and your feet seem to stick in the mud so that you can't run. It is a very frightful sort of dream. And this adventure the little ones had got into was surely a frightful peril.

The hissing gander, his neck outstretched and his bill wide open, followed the two children with every evidence of wishing to strike them. His flapping wings were as powerful, it seemed, as those of the big sea-eagle that had been caught aboard ship coming down from Boston, and Mun Bun and Margy remembered that creature very vividly.

Others of the flock of geese came on, too. As long as the grains of corn kept dropping from Margy's dish, the ravenous geese would follow, even if they were not savage, as their leader was.

The chubby legs of the two children hardly kept them ahead of the gander's bill. They shrieked at the top of their voices. But for once none of the innumerable colored folks was in sight. Even their friend, the gardener, had disappeared since Mun Bun and Margy had come down to the goose pen.

"Help! Help us!" cried Margy, looking to the world in general to assist.

"Muvver! Muvver!" cried Mun Bun, who held an unshaken belief that Mother Bunker must be always at hand and able to rescue him from any trouble.

Mun Bun thought he felt the cold, hard bill of the gander at his bare legs. He ran so hard that he lost his breath, somewhere. He couldn't even pant, and as for calling out for help again, that was impossible!

Margy dragged him on a few steps, for she was quite strong for a little girl. But she knew that she was overtaken. There was no help for it. The goosey-goosey-gander was going to eat them up!

But if no human being heard the two children in their distress, there was a creature that did. Bobo, the big old hound, who was only chained to his house at night or when Mr. Armatage did not want him following the mules about the plantation, came out of his kennel and stared down the hill. He observed the running and screaming children, and he likewise saw the gander who was his old enemy. They had had many a tilt before, for the gander believed that everything that came near his flock meant mischief.

Bobo's red eyes expanded and the ruff on the back of his neck began to rise. He uttered a low, reverberating bark. It was almost a growl and it sounded threatening. He dashed down the hill with great leaps.

Mun Bun finally pitched over on his face, dragging Margy with him. Margy's corn went spinning about her and the geese fairly scrambled over the two crying children to get at the corn. Perhaps this helped Mun Bun and his sister some, although they did not think so at the moment. At least, while his family scrambled for the grains of corn the gander could not get at the brother and sister to strike them.

And then great Bobo appeared. He bounded into the middle of the flock and knocked them every-which-way with his great paws. He thrust his muzzle under the hissing gander and sent him over on his back, where he lay and flapped his webbed feet ridiculously. And he did not hiss any more. He "honked" for help.

Mun Bun and Margy scarcely knew that they were saved until Bobo thrust his cold, wet muzzle into first one face and then the other of the two little Bunkers. They had become so used to Aunt Jo's great Dane doing that that Bobo's affectionate act did not alarm them.

"The goosey-goosey-gander's gone, Margy!" stammered Mun Bun. "I told you I wouldn't let him bite you."

Whether his sister was much impressed by this statement or not, is not known. However that might be, she fondled Bobo and got upon her feet as quickly as Mun Bun arose.

"Isn't he a good old dog?" cooed Margy.

"He's pretty good I think. But - but let's come away from that goosey-goosey-gander."

Bobo gave a jump and a bark at the gander, and the latter, which had now climbed to its webbed feet, scurried away, the flock following him. It was then, while the two children were fondling Bobo, who liked to have his long ears pulled by a gentle hand, that Russ and Rose Bunker came upon the scene.

Russ and Rose had been down to the burned cabin and had brought away all their letters to Sneezer Meiggs. If the colored boy had never learned to read writing, there was no use in leaving the notices there. So Russ had said, and Rose agreed with him.

"Oh, my dears!" Rose cried out when she saw the little ones so mussed up and with tear-stained faces, "what has happened to you?"

"Don't be afraid of Bobo," said Russ, running too. "He won't hurt you."

"He hurted the goosey-goosey-gander," declared Mun Bun confidently. "He dug his head under the goosey-goosey-gander and flunged him right over on his back."

"But he wouldn't hurt you," declared Rose.

"No," explained Margy. "Bobo came to help us when the gander wanted to bite our legs. At any rate he wanted to bite Mun Bun's legs."

"'Twas your legs he was after, Margy," declared the little fellow, flushing. "I wouldn't let the goosey-goosey-gander bite mine."

"Anyhow," said Margy, "he chased us. And all his hens came too. And Bobo saw him and he came down and drove them off. See! That gander is hissing at us now."

"Bobo is a brave dog," cried Rose, patting the hound.

"He is pretty good, I think," declared Mun Bun. "But next time I go down to that goose place I am going to have a big stick."

"The next time," advised Russ, "don't you go there at all unless Daddy Bunker is with you. I'd be afraid of that old gander myself."

"Oh, would you?" cried the little boy, greatly relieved. "We-ell, I was a teeny bit scared myself."

The children - all nine of them - spent much of their time in Mammy June's room. The old colored woman had ways of keeping them interested and quiet that Mrs. Armatage proclaimed she could not understand. Mother Bunker understood the charm Mammy worked far better.

Mammy June loved children, high and low, rich and poor, good and bad, just so they were children. Therefore, Mammy June could manage them. Russ and Rose, finding themselves mistaken in their first attempt to relieve the old woman's anxiety about her son, wondered in private what they could do to let the absent Sneezer know where his mother was, and how much she wanted to see him.

Russ and Rose Bunker were quite used to thinking things out for themselves. Of course, there were times when Russ had to go to Daddy Bunker for help and his sister had to confess to Mother Bunker that she did not know what to do. For instance, that adventure of Russ's with the sailor-boy aboard the steamship.

But this matter of helping Mammy June's son to find his mother, if by chance he came back to the site of the burned cabin, was solely their own affair, and Russ and Rose realized the fact.

"We ought to be able to do something about it ourselves," declared Russ to his sister. "I'm going to ask Mammy June again if she is sure Sneezer can't read a word of writing."

This he did. Mammy June shook her head somewhat sadly.

"Dat boy always have to wo'k," she said. "When first he went away he sent me back money by mail. The man he wo'ked for sent it. Then Sneezer lost his job. But he never learnt to read hand-writin'. Much as he could do to spell out the big print on the front of the newspapers. That's surely so!"

Rose suddenly thought of something - and perhaps it was not a foolish idea at that.

"Oh, Mammy!" she cried, "can your boy read newspaper print?"

"Sure can. De big print. What yo' call de haidlines in big print.

Sure can."

"Oh!" murmured Rose, and she dragged Russ away to confer with him in secret.

Laura Lee Hope

CHAPTER XXII

THE STRANGE CRY

Rose Bunker's idea was too good to tell in general. Some ideas are too good to keep; but Russ and Rose decided that this one was not in that class. They determined to tell nobody - not even Mammy June or Daddy or Mother Bunker - about what they proposed to do to help the old colored woman.

They had tried once, and failed. And Philly and Alice and Frane, Junior, had laughed at them. Now they proposed to do what Rose had thought of, and keep it secret from everybody.

"Of course," Rose said, "nothing may come of it."

"But that won't be your fault, Rose," said her brother. "It is a perfectly scrumptious idea."

"Do you think so?" asked Rose, much pleased by this frank praise.

"Sure I do. And we'll do it to-night. Then the Armatages won't know and - and laugh at us."

For they had found Philly and Alice and Frane, Junior, rather trying. Not having their childish imaginations so well developed as the six little Bunkers had, the children of the plantation were altogether too matter-of-fact. Many childish plays that the Bunkers enjoyed did not appeal to their little hosts at all.

For instance, when Russ invented some brand new and charming, simple play for all to join in, Philly and Alice and Frane just drifted away and would have nothing to do with it. They were too polite to criticize; but Russ knew that the Armatage children felt themselves "too grown up" to be interested in the building of a steamboat or the driving of an imaginary motor-car.

His little brothers and sisters, however, were constantly teasing Russ to make something new. They enjoyed traveling in reality so much, did the six little Bunkers, that, as Daddy laughingly said, traveling in a wheelbarrow would have amused them.

So this day when Russ made a whole freight train with empty chicken coops, with a caboose at the end and a big engine in front, only Frane took an interest in it aside from the Bunkers themselves. And perhaps his interest was, only held because Russ agreed to make him the engineer while Laddie was fireman.

As for Russ himself, he was the conductor at the end of the long train. He had to explain very plainly that of course a freight train had a conductor. Every train had to have a "skipper" just like a boat. A railroad man had explained all that to Russ Bunker when the family was on its way to Cowboy Jack's early in the autumn.

"And you-all," said Russ, copying Frane's speech, speaking to the little ones and Rose, "must stay back here with me and be brakemen. When we need the handbrakes, I'll tell you, and you run forward over the coops - I mean the cars - and set the brakes."

"But suppose we get flung off?" asked Vi.

"That you must not do," said her older brother sternly. "If the train is going fast you might get a broken leg. Or if it is going

Laura Lee Hope

around a curve it would be worse. You must be careful."

"I think this is a dangerous play," said Vi hopefully. There was nobody really more daring than Vi.

The two Armatage girls tried to coax Rose away from the "train"; but Rose liked to play with her brothers and sisters, and she knew that Mother Bunker expected her to. So she excused herself to Philly and Alice.

Unfortunately they took some offense at this. That evening after supper Rose found herself ignored by Phillis and Alice Armatage. At another time this ungenerous act might have hurt the oldest Bunker girl. But she and Russ had their secret plans to carry through, and Rose was glad to get away with her brother in a room where nobody would disturb them.

Again Russ had broken up pasteboard boxes, and he had pen and ink. To make new signs all in "big print" to stick up at the site of Mammy June's burned cabin was more of a task than merely writing them. This was Rose's bright idea. Russ did not deny her powers of invention.

They printed four good signs. Oh, the letters were large and black!

"They ought to be," Russ said. "We've used 'most half a bottle of ink."

"Don't let's tell Philly or any of them," said Rose. "They laugh at so many things we do."

"All right," agreed Russ, although he was less sensitive about being laughed at than his sister.

But this habit the young Armatages had of laughing at what the little Bunkers did caused all the trouble on this night. And it was a night that all of the children and most of the grown folks, too, would be likely to remember.

The Armatage children knew a great deal more about the plantation and the country surrounding it than the Bunkers did. That was only natural. Philly or Alice or Frane, Junior, would not have started off secretly, as Russ and Rose Bunker did, after nine o'clock at night to go down to the place where old Mammy June's cabin had been burned.

To tell the truth, the Armatage children had associated so much with the colored folks about the plantation that they were inclined to believe that there might be such things as "ha'nts." The little Bunkers had heard of "ghosts"; but they looked on such things as being like fairies - something to half-believe in, and shiver about, all the time knowing that they were not real.

So Russ and Rose had no actual fear of haunts when they started down the cart-path toward the wide brook where Russ had had his first adventure catching the big fish.

The colored folks were all at home in their quarters; and although it was a starlight night they were having no celebration. Everything about the plantation seemed particularly quiet. And no sounds at first came to the ears of the brother and sister from the forest.

As they approached the place for which they aimed however there came suddenly a mournful screech from the woods - a sound that seemed to linger longer in their hearing than any strange noise Russ and Rose had ever heard. The brother and sister stopped, frightened indeed, and clung to each other.

"Oh! What's that?" murmured Rose.

"It - it's maybe an owl," returned Russ, trying to think of the most harmless creature that made a noise at night.

"I never heard an owl howl like that," whispered his sister.

"Aw, Rose! owls don't howl. It's wolves that howl - or coyotes such as we saw at Cowboy Jack's. Don't you remember the coyote caught in the trap that you thought was a dog?"

Rose's mind would not be drawn from the thing in question. She said, quite as fearfully:

"Maybe this is a wolf, Russ."

"Of course not," declared the boy trying to speak bravely. "There aren't any wolves in this part of the country. I asked Frane, Junior."

But there was evidently a savage creature here that Russ Bunker had known nothing about, for now it cried out again! Its long, quavering note echoed through the woods and made the boy and girl stand again and shiver.

"I - I guess it isn't any animal after all," said Rose suddenly, and speaking with some relief. "That's a woman. Of course it is. But she must be lost, or something bad has happened to her. Oh, Russ!" she added, suddenly seizing her brother once more. "I know what it must be. And they are almost always ladies, so Phillis says."

"What's that?" demanded Russ, puzzled.

"It's a ha'nt! It's a lady ha'nt! I do believe it must be!"

"Aw, Rose, what you talking about?" demanded her brother, yet secretly quite as much troubled by the strange, eerie sound as she was. "You know that haunts are only make-believe."

"We-ell!" sighed Rose, "maybe that's only a make-believe sound we hear. But - but I don't like it. There!"

For a third time the screech was repeated. It seemed nearer. Russ could not be confident that it was "make-believe." The strange sound seemed very real indeed.

CHAPTER XXIII

A FOUR-LEGGED GHOST

"I don't like that noise a bit," whispered Rose, standing close to her brother. "It - it makes me all shivery."

"But, if it is only just a woman calling -"

"There must be something awful the matter with her, if she has to scream like that," declared Rose.

As they did not hear the noise again for a little while, both of them plucked up courage, and they went on to the burned cabin. The sticks they had set up were still standing. Russ fastened each of the four pasteboard "letters" to a stick at the four corners of Mammy June's ruined house.

There was light enough from the stars for the two children to see quite plainly what they were about. Rose, however, was looking all about them while Russ did the work of setting up the printed signs for Sneezer Meiggs to see if he came home unexpectedly.

"What do you expect to see, Rose?" demanded her brother loftily.

"I don't know. Philly says ha'nts are all in white."

"I don't see anything very white around here," rejoined Russ.

"But there are so many colored folks, perhaps some of the ha'nts might be black," suggested Rose. "Then we wouldn't see them very well in the shadows."

"I don't believe -" began Russ.

The strange shriek was again heard. Russ stopped in his speech. Rose uttered a sharp cry. The screech - and it did sound like a woman's voice, the voice of a woman in fearful pain or fright - seemed very near them.

"It's right over there in that patch of woods," said Russ. "I guess she is lost - or something."

"Do you believe it is only a lady and not a ha'nt, Russ?" demanded his sister.

"Of course it isn't a ha'nt! Such things can't be! And if it was a ghost, a ghost is nothing but air, and how could air have such a voice as that?"

This reasoning seemed to close the argument. Rose felt that her brother must be right. Besides, Russ went right on talking, and talking very bravely.

"I think we ought to see what the matter is with her, Rose. She is in trouble - maybe she is lost and scared."

"So am I scared," murmured Rose.

"But think how much more you would be scared," her brother said seriously, "if you were in those woods alone and didn't know that there was anybody else near."

"I wouldn't make so much fuss about it," muttered Rose, for she suspected the thought in Russ Bunker's mind and she was really too scared to approve of it at once.

"We've got to find her," said the boy impressively.

"Now, Russ!" almost wailed Rose, "you wouldn't go into those woods? Aren't you scared?"

"Of course I'm scared," said Russ. "Who wouldn't be? But just because I am scared I know the woman must be even more scared. She's got to be taken out of the woods and shown where the big house is. Or, if she is a colored lady, we'll take her to the quarters."

"I - I wish Daddy was here," ventured Rose.

"But he isn't here," said Russ, with some vexation. "So we've got to find the woman by ourselves."

"Oh, dear!" murmured Rose.

But she would not let Russ go alone into the patch of forest behind the site of Mammy June's burned cabin; nor did she feel like remaining alone in the clearing. Russ picked up a good sized stick and started toward the woods.

"Let's shout when we get to the edge," whispered Rose.

They did so; but, really, their voices sounded very faint indeed. No reply came. It was several minutes after, and Russ and Rose were quite a distance into the woods and following what seemed to be a half-grown-over path, before the "woman" screamed again.

"Goodness! How hateful that sounds!" cried Rose.

"I guess she is more scared than we are," ventured Russ. "What do you think?"

"I think I'd like to be back at the house," answered Rose.

But Russ would not agree with her. As he went on he grew more confident. They did not see even a rabbit. And Russ and Rose knew that rabbits were often out at night.

If they had but known it, the awful screech that so disturbed them, disturbed the rabbits and the other small fry of the woods much more. At the sound of that terrible hunger-cry all the rabbits, and hares, and birds that nested on the ground or in trees, trembled.

But Russ seemed to grow braver by the minute. And Rose of course could not fail to be inspired by his show of courage. They walked along the path hand in hand, and although they did not speak much for the next few moments, when they did speak it was quite cheerfully.

"I wish she would yell again," said Russ at last. "For we must be getting near to where she was."

"We-ell, if she isn't a ghost -"

Just then the silence of the wood was broken again by the cry. The boy and the girl halted involuntarily. No matter how brave Russ might appear to be, there was a tone to that scream that made shivers go up and down his back.

"Oh, Russ!" cried Rose.

"Oh, Rose!" stammered her brother.

The scream came from so near that it seemed worse than before. And now Russ was shaken in his proclaimed opinion. It did not seem that any woman, no matter how great her distress might be, could make such a terrible sound.

"I guess we'd better go back," confessed Russ after a minute.

Rose was eager to do so. They turned and, hand in hand, began to run. And in their haste they somehow missed the path they had been following. Or else, it had not been a path at all.

At least, after running so far that they should have reached the burned cabin they came out into quite a different clearing! They both knew that they had missed the way, for in this clearing stood a little cabin with a pitched roof that neither of the Bunker children had ever seen before. Nor was the wide brook in sight.

"I guess we've got turned around," Russ said, trying to hide his disappointment and fear from his sister. "We've got to go back, Rose."

"Do you know which is back?" she asked.

"We've got to hunt for that old path."

"Don't you leave me, Russ Bunker!" cried Rose, as her brother started away.

And just then both of them saw the tawny, long tailed, slinking beast in the edge of the thicket.

"Oh! It's a bear!" shrieked Rose.

"Bears don't look like that," gasped Russ, staring at the great, glowing eyes of the animal. "It looks more like a cat."

"There never was a cat as big as that, Russ Bunker, and you know it!"

"Come on, Rose," said her brother promptly. "We'll go into that house and shut the door. It can't get us then, whatever it is."

In a moment the two children had dashed into the cabin and pulled to the swinging door. The door had a lock on the outside, and when Russ banged the door shut he heard the lock snap.

"Now it can't get at us!" cried Russ with some satisfaction. "We're safe."

Laura Lee Hope

"But - but I don't like this old house, Russ Bunker," complained Rose. "There is no window."

"All the better," was the brave reply. "That cat can't get at us."

Then the screech sounded again and the boy and girl clung together while the sound echoed through the lonesome timber.

"It's that thing that makes the noise," whispered Rose. "Oh, Russ! If Daddy Bunker doesn't come after us, maybe it will tear the house down."

"It can't," declared Russ.

"How do you know it can't?"

"Why, cats - even big ones - don't tear houses to pieces, Rose. You know they don't! We'll be safe as long as we stay in this place."

"But how long shall we have to stay here?"

"Until that thing goes away," said Russ confidently.

"And maybe it won't go away at all. We'll have to stay here till the folks come to find us, Russ. I - I want - my mo-mother!"

"Now, Rose Bunker, don't be a baby!" said her brother. "That thing can't get at us in here -"

Just then something thumped heavily on the roof of the hut. Russ could not say another word. They heard the great claws of the big cat scratching at the roof boards.

Rose screamed again and this time her brother's voice joined with hers in a hopeless cry for help.

CHAPTER XXIV

AN EXCITING TIME

Russ and Rose Bunker had slipped out of the house on the hill without saying a word to anybody as to where they were going. Since coming to the Meiggs Plantation there had been a certain amount of laxness in regard to what the children did. They had a freedom that Mother Bunker never allowed when they were at home.

Because the Armatage children went and came as they wished, the little Bunkers began to do likewise. The house was so big, too, that the children might be playing a long way from the room in which their mother and father and Mr. Frane Armatage and his wife sat.

The servants who were supposed to keep some watch upon the children were now all in the quarters. Servants in the South seldom sleep in "the big house." And perhaps Mother Bunker forgot this fact.

At any rate, when she came to look for her brood late in the evening she found the four little ones fast asleep in their beds, as she had expected them to be. But Rose was not with Phillis and Alice Armatage, and Russ's bed was likewise empty.

"Where are those children?" Mother Bunker demanded of Daddy, when she had run downstairs again. "Do you know? They should be in bed."

"They were in the library earlier in the evening," Mrs. Armatage said. "I think they were writing again."

"Writing?" repeated Mother Bunker. "Making more of those signs to set up at the burned house?"

Mr. Armatage chuckled. "Those won't do much good. Sneezer never could read writing."

"Let us ask Mammy. Rose and Russ may be with her," suggested Mrs. Armatage.

Upstairs went the two ladies and into Mammy June's room. There was a night light burning there, but nobody was with the old woman.

"Lawsy me!" exclaimed the old nurse when Mrs. Bunker asked her. "I ain't seen them childern since I had my supper. No'm. They ain't been here."

The house was searched from cellar to garret by the two gentlemen. Meanwhile the anxious mother and her hostess went to the library. Russ had left there some spoiled sheets of cardboard with some of the letters printed on them. It was easy to see the attempt he and Rose had made to print plainly a notice to Sneezer, Mammy June's absent son, telling him that his mother was at the big house.

"The dear things!" said Mrs. Armatage. "Your boy and girl are very kind, Mrs. Bunker. They want to relieve Mammy's trouble."

"They have gone down there to-night to stick up those signs!" cried Mrs. Bunker, inspired by a new thought.

"Well, I reckon nothing will hurt 'em," said her friend soothingly. "I'll tell Mr. Armatage and he will go down there and get them."

This idea impressed both the men when they came back from their unsuccessful search of the house.

The two men walked briskly along the trail to the burned cabin. The stars gave them light enough to see all about the clearing when they arrived. Not a sign of Russ or Rose did they find.

"Do you suppose they went home some other way?" asked Daddy Bunker.

"I don't know. I hope they haven't wandered into the thicket."

As Mr. Armatage spoke both men heard the terrible scream that had first startled Russ and Rose. Mr. Bunker fairly jumped.

"That can't be the children!" he ejaculated.

The way his companion looked at him told the children's father a good deal. Mr. Bunker seized Mr. Armatage's arm.

"Tell me! What is it?" he asked.

"Something that hasn't been heard around here for years," said the planter, his voice trembling a little. "It's the cry of a panther."

Mr. Bunker, although he was practically a city man, had hunted a good deal and had been in the wilder parts of the country very often. He knew how terribly dangerous a panther might be on occasion; but he likewise knew that ordinarily they would not attack human beings. Two little children lost in the woods in which a panther was roaming up and down was, however, a fearful thing.

"Get a gun and the hands!" exclaimed Mr. Bunker. "If Russ and Rose have mistaken the way home, and are in that timber, they may be in peril."

Mr. Armatage started off on a run for the quarters. He knew that some of his hands had guns, and the quarters were nearer than the big house.

Daddy Bunker, although he was unarmed, started directly into the woods, trying to mark his course by the repeated screams of the hungry panther. He might have been lost himself, for there was not much light to mark the way; but Daddy Bunker could judge the situation of the screaming panther much better than Russ and Rose had been able to.

He hurried on, gripping a good-sized club that he had found. But, of course, he knew better than to attack a panther with a club. He might throw the stick at the animal, however, and frighten it away.

Russ and Rose had gone a long way into the thicket. The panther did not scream often. So Daddy Bunker did not make much progress in the right direction. By and by he had to stop and wait for help, or for the panther to scream again.

He heard finally many voices at the edge of the thicket. Then he began to see the blaze of torches. A party of colored people - men and boys - with torches and guns, followed Mr. Armatage.

In addition, all the hunting dogs on the plantation were scouring the timber. Bobo, the big hound, was at the head of this pack. He struck the scent of the panther at last, and his long and mournful howl was almost as awe-inspiring as the cry of the panther.

"Come on, Bunker!" shouted Mr. Armatage, when the party had overtaken the Northern man. "The dogs are the best leaders. Bobo has got a scent for any kind of trail. Come on!"

The negroes shouted and swung their torches. Perhaps they made so much noise and had so many lights because they somewhat feared the "ha'nts" that many of them talked about and believed in.

But the two white men were not thinking of ghosts. They feared what might have happened to the two children if they had met the panther.

Just at this time, too, Russ and Rose were not thinking of ghosts. The panther was not at all ghostly. He had four great paws, each armed with claws that seemed quite capable of tearing to pieces the roof boards of the cabin the children had taken refuge in.

"He'll get to us! He will! He will!" Rose cried over and over.

"No, he won't," said her brother, but his voice trembled. "I - I don't see how he can."

"Let's run out again while he's on the roof, and run home," said Rose.

"We don't know the way home," objected her brother.

"We can find it. I don't want to be shut up here with that cat."

"It's not so bad. He hasn't got in yet."

But Rose ran to the door, and then she made another discovery that added to her fright. The door could not be opened! The spring lock on the outside had snapped and there was no way of springing the bolt from inside the shack.

"Now see what we've done!" she wailed. "Russ Bunker! we are shut into the place, and can't get out, and that thing will come down and claw us all to pieces."

With this Rose cast herself upon the ground and could not be comforted. In fact, at the moment, Russ could not think of a word to say that would comfort his sister. He was just as much frightened as Rose was.

Laura Lee Hope

CHAPTER XXV

THAT PIGEON WING

Greatly as the two little Bunkers were alarmed, and as much as their father and Mr. Armatage worried about their safety, they really were not so very badly off. Not only were the roof boards of the hut in which Russ and Rose had taken refuge sound, but soon the panther stopped clawing at the boards.

It heard the crowd of men coming and the baying of the hounds. It stood up, stretched its neck as it listened, snarled a defiance at Bobo and his mates, and then leaped into the nearest tree and so away, from tree to tree, into the deeper fastnesses of the wood.

The dogs might follow the scent of the panther on the ground to the clearing where the hut stood; but beyond that place they could not follow, for the wary cat had left no trail upon the ground.

At first, when the dogs came baying to the spot, Russ and Rose were even more frightened than before. The dogs' voices sounded very savage. But soon Bobo smelled the children out and leaped, whining, against the door of the cabin. He was doing that when Daddy Bunker and Mr. Armatage and the negroes reached the clearing.

"The creature is in that hut," said Daddy Bunker.

"Not much!" returned his friend. "Bobo would not make those sounds if it was a panther. Mr. Panther has beat it through the trees. It is something else in the charcoal burner's hut. Come on!"

He strode over to the door, snapped back the lock, and threw the door open. The torchlight flooded the interior of the place and revealed Russ and Rose Bunker, still fearful, clinging to each other as they crouched in a corner of the hut.

"Well!" exclaimed Daddy Bunker. "Of all the children that ever were born, you two manage to get into the greatest adventures! What are you doing here?"

"A big cat chased us in here, Daddy," said Russ.

"And he tried to get at us through the roof," added Rose.

Daddy Bunker and Mr. Armatage looked at each other pretty seriously.

"We didn't get here a minute too soon," said the planter.

"I believe you," returned Mr. Bunker gravely. "This might have been a very serious affair."

But in the morning, after Russ and Rose were refreshed by sleep and had told the particulars of their adventure at the breakfast table, the youngsters really took pride in what had happened to them. The smaller children looked upon Russ and Rose as being very wonderful.

"What would you have done, Russ, if that big cat had got into the house with you and Rose?" Vi asked.

"But he didn't," was the boy's reply.

"Well, if he had what would you have done?"

But that proved to be another question that Vi Bunker never got answered. This was so often the case!

"So you thought it was a ghost at first, and then it turned out to be a big cat," Laddie said to Rose. "I think I could make up a riddle about that."

"All right," said Rose, with a sigh. "You can make up all the riddles you want to about it. Making a riddle about a panther is lots better than being chased by one."

Laddie, however, did not make the riddle. In fact he forgot all about it in the excitement of what directly followed the rescue of Russ and Rose from the wild animal. Mr. Bunker felt so happy about the recovery of the two children that he determined to do something nice for the colored people who had so enthusiastically aided in hunting for Russ and Rose.

"Let 'em have another big dance and dinner, such as they had Christmas eve," Mr. Bunker suggested to the planter. "I'll pay the bill."

"Just as you say, Charley," agreed Mr. Armatage. "That will please 'em all about as much as anything you could think of. I'll get some kind of music for them to dance by, and we'll all go down and watch 'em. Your young ones certainly do like dancing."

This was true. And especially was Russ Bunker anxious to learn to dance as some of the colored boys did. He was constantly practising the funny pigeon wing that he had seen Sam do in Aunt Jo's kitchen, in Boston. But the white boy could not get it just right.

"Never mind, Russ," Laddie said approvingly, "you do it better and better all the time. I guess you can do it by and by - three or four years from now, maybe." But three or four years seemed a long time to Russ.

When they went down to the quarters the evening of the party Russ determined to try to dance as well as Frane, Junior, and the negro boys.

Mammy June was much better now, and she was up and about. To please her Mr. Armatage had a phaeton brought around and the old nurse was driven to the scene of the celebration. Mun Bun and Margy rode in the phaeton with Mammy June and were very proud of this particular honor.

The old nurse was loved by everybody on the plantation, both white and black. Mother Bunker said that Mammy held "quite a levee" at the quarters, sitting in state in her phaeton where she could see all that went on.

The dinner was what the negroes called a barbecue. The six little Bunkers had never seen such a feast before, for this that their father gave them was even more elaborate than the dinner the planter had given his hands at Christmas.

There was a great fire in a pit, and over this fire a whole pig was roasted on a spit, and poultry, and 'possums that the boys had killed, and rabbits. There were sweet potatoes, of course. How the little Northerners liked them! The white children had a table to themselves and ate as heartily as their colored friends.

Then a place was cleared for the dancing. Mammy June's phaeton was drawn to the edge of this dance floor. The music struck up, and there was a general rush for partners.

After a while the dancers got more excited, and many of them danced alone, "showing off," Frane, Junior, said. They did have the funniest steps! Russ Bunker was highly delighted with this kind of dancing.

"Now let me! Let me dance!" he cried, starting out from his seat near Mammy June. "A boy showed me in Boston how to cut a pigeon wing. I guess I can do it now."

"You can't cut no pigeon wing, w'ite boy," said 'Lias, Mammy's grandson.

"I can try," said Russ bravely, and he danced with much vigor for several minutes.

"Oh, my, he done cut Sneezer's pigeon wing!" cried one of the darkies presently.

"What's dat? Cut Sneezer's pigeon wing?" cried Mammy June, sitting up to watch Russ more closely.

"Dat's jest what he's doin'."

Russ continued to dance, and did his best to imitate the colored boy at Aunt Jo's house. He was hard at it when Mammy June, with her eyes almost popping out of her head, cried:

"For de lan's sake, boy, come here! I want to ask you sumpin."

Russ was in the midst of cutting the pigeon wing again, and this time he was fortunate enough to imitate Sam in almost every particular. Then he stopped and walked over to the old colored woman's side.

"How come you try to do it that way, Russ Bunker?" asked Mammy June as Russ approached the phaeton. "I ain't never seen you do that before. Who showed you?"

"Sam. The boy in Boston. He said he was called after his Uncle Sam. He came from down South here, you know, Mammy."

"Was he a cullud boy?" demanded the old woman earnestly.

"Of course he was. Or he couldn't dance this way," and Russ tried to cut the pigeon wing again.

"Wait! Wait!" gasped the old woman. "Tell me mo' about that boy who showed you. You ain't got it right. But dat's the way my Sneezer done it. Only he knows just how."

"Why, Mammy June!" cried Rose, "you don't suppose that Sam can dance just like your Sneezer?"

The old nurse was wiping the tears from her cheeks. Her voice was much choked with emotion as well. Mrs. Bunker came over to see what the matter was.

"Yo' please tell me, Ma'am, all about dat boy dese children say was in Boston? Please, Ma'am! Ain't nobody know how to dance dat way but Sneezer. And he didn't like his name, Ebenezer Caliper Spotiswood Meiggs. No'm, he didn't like it at all, 'cause we-all shortened it to Sneezer.

"He had an Uncle Sam, too. My brudder. Lives in Birmingham. Sneezer always said he wisht he'd been born wid a name like Uncle Sam."

"Perhaps it is the same boy," Mother Bunker said kindly. "Tell me just how Ebenezer looks, Mammy June. Then I can be sure."

From the way Mammy described her youngest son, even the children recognized him as Sam the chore boy at Aunt Jo's in Boston. Mun Bun and Margy, when the matter was quite settled that Sam was Sneezer, began to take great pride in the fact that it was their bright eyes that had first spied the colored boy walking in the snow and had been the first to invite him into Aunt Jo's house.

"He will be there when we go to Boston again, Mammy June," Rose said, warmly. "And Daddy and Mother will send him home to you. I guess he'll be glad to come. Only, maybe you'd better stop calling him Sneezer. He likes Sam best."

"Sure enough, honey," cried Mammy June, "I'll call him

anything he likes 'long as he comes home and stays home with me. Yes, indeedy! I'd call him Julius Caesar Mark Antony Meiggs, if he wants I should."

"But maybe," said Russ thoughtfully, "he wouldn't like that name any better than the other. I know I shouldn't."

In a short time it was a settled matter that Mammy June's lost boy would return. For she could tell Mrs. Bunker so many things about the absent one that there was not a shadow of a doubt that the Sam working for Aunt Jo would prove to be Mammy June's boy.

The holidays on the Meiggs Plantation ended, therefore, all the more pleasantly because of this discovery. The plantation was a fine place to be on, so the six little Bunkers thought. But when Daddy Bunker announced that his business with his old friend, the planter, was satisfactorily completed, the children were not sorry to think of returning North.

"This doesn't seem like winter at all down here," said Russ. "We want to slide downhill, and roll snowballs, and make snowmen."

"And it is nice to go sleigh riding," Rose added. "They never can do that on the Meiggs Plantation."

"But you can make riddles here," put in Laddie.

Vi might have added that she could ask questions anywhere!

As for Margy and Mun Bun, they were contented to go anywhere that Mother Bunker and Daddy went. Something exciting was always happening to all of the six little Bunkers. But we will let you guess, with Russ and Rose and Vi and Laddie and Margy and Mun Bun, where the next exciting adventures of the half dozen youngsters from Pineville will take place.

Then came the time to leave the plantation. The children had many little keepsakes to take home with them and they promised to send other keepsakes to the Armatage children as soon as they got back to Pineville.

"It's been just the nicest outing that ever could be!" said Rose, when the good-byes were being spoken. "I'm sure I'll never forget this lovely place."

"I's coming back some day if they want me," put in Mun Bun quickly. And at this everybody smiled.

Then all climbed into the automobile which was to take them to the railroad station. There was a honk of the horn, and amid the waving of hands and a hearty cheer, the six little Bunkers and their parents started on their journey for home.

Choose from Thousands of 1stWorldLibrary Classics By

A. M. Barnard
Ada Leverson
Adolphus William Ward
Aesop
Agatha Christie
Alexander Aaronsohn
Alexander Kielland
Alexandre Dumas
Alfred Gatty
Alfred Ollivant
Alice Duer Miller
Alice Turner Curtis
Alice Dunbar
Allen Chapman
Ambrose Bierce
Amelia E. Barr
Amory H. Bradford
Andrew Lang
Andrew McFarland Davis
Andy Adams
Anna Alice Chapin
Anna Sewell
Annie Besant
Annie Hamilton Donnell
Annie Payson Call
Annie Roe Carr
Annonaymous
Anton Chekhov
Arnold Bennett
Arthur Conan Doyle
Arthur M. Winfield
Arthur Ransome
Arthur Schnitzler
Atticus
B.H. Baden-Powell
B. M. Bower
B. C. Chatterjee
Baroness Emmuska Orczy
Baroness Orczy
Basil King
Bayard Taylor
Ben Macomber
Bertha Muzzy Bower
Bjornstjerne Bjornson
Booth Tarkington
Boyd Cable
Bram Stoker
C. Collodi
C. E. Orr

C. M. Ingleby
Carolyn Wells
Catherine Parr Traill
Charles A. Eastman
Charles Amory Beach
Charles Dickens
Charles Dudley Warner
Charles Farrar Browne
Charles Ives
Charles Kingsley
Charles Klein
Charles Hanson Towne
Charles Lathrop Pack
Charles Romyn Dake
Charles Whibley
Charles Willing Beale
Charlotte M. Braeme
Charlotte M. Yonge
Charlotte Perkins Stetson
Clair W. Hayes
Clarence Day Jr.
Clarence E. Mulford
Clemence Housman
Confucius
Coningsby Dawson
Cornelis DeWitt Wilcox
Cyril Burleigh
D. H. Lawrence
Daniel Defoe
David Garnett
Dinah Craik
Don Carlos Janes
Donald Keyhoe
Dorothy Kilner
Dougan Clark
Douglas Fairbanks
E. Nesbit
E.P.Roe
E. Phillips Oppenheim
Earl Barnes
Edgar Rice Burroughs
Edith Van Dyne
Edith Wharton
Edward Everett Hale
Edward J. O'Biren
Edward S. Ellis
Edwin L. Arnold
Eleanor Atkins
Eliot Gregory

Elizabeth Gaskell
Elizabeth McCracken
Elizabeth Von Arnim
Ellem Key
Emerson Hough
Emilie F. Carlen
Emily Dickinson
Enid Bagnold
Enilor Macartney Lane
Erasmus W. Jones
Ernie Howard Pie
Ethel May Dell
Ethel Turner
Ethel Watts Mumford
Eugenie Foa
Eugene Wood
Eustace Hale Ball
Evelyn Everett-green
Everard Cotes
F. H. Cheley
F. J. Cross
F. Marion Crawford
Federick Austin Ogg
Ferdinand Ossendowski
Francis Bacon
Francis Darwin
Frances Hodgson Burnett
Frances Parkinson Keyes
Frank Gee Patchin
Frank Harris
Frank Jewett Mather
Frank L. Packard
Frank V. Webster
Frederic Stewart Isham
Frederick Trevor Hill
Frederick Winslow Taylor
Friedrich Kerst
Friedrich Nietzsche
Fyodor Dostoyevsky
G.A. Henty
G.K. Chesterton
Gabrielle E. Jackson
Garrett P. Serviss
Gaston Leroux
George A. Warren
George Ade
Geroge Bernard Shaw
George Durston
George Ebers

George Eliot
George Gissing
George MacDonald
George Meredith
George Orwell
George Sylvester Viereck
George Tucker
George W. Cable
George Wharton James
Gertrude Atherton
Gordon Casserly
Grace E. King
Grace Gallatin
Grace Greenwood
Grant Allen
Guillermo A. Sherwell
Gulielma Zollinger
Gustav Flaubert
H. A. Cody
H. B. Irving
H.C. Bailey
H. G. Wells
H. H. Munro
H. Irving Hancock
H. Rider Haggard
H. W. C. Davis
Haldeman Julius
Hall Caine
Hamilton Wright Mabie
Hans Christian Andersen
Harold Avery
Harold McGrath
Harriet Beecher Stowe
Harry Castlemon
Harry Coghill
Harry Houidini
Hayden Carruth
Helent Hunt Jackson
Helen Nicolay
Hendrik Conscience
Hendy David Thoreau
Henri Barbusse
Henrik Ibsen
Henry Adams
Henry Ford
Henry Frost
Henry James
Henry Jones Ford
Henry Seton Merriman
Henry W Longfellow
Herbert A. Giles

Herbert Carter
Herbert N. Casson
Herman Hesse
Hildegard G. Frey
Homer
Honore De Balzac
Horace B. Day
Horace Walpole
Horatio Alger Jr.
Howard Pyle
Howard R. Garis
Hugh Lofting
Hugh Walpole
Humphry Ward
Ian Maclaren
Inez Haynes Gillmore
Irving Bacheller
Isabel Hornibrook
Israel Abrahams
Ivan Turgenev
J.G.Austin
J. Henri Fabre
J. M. Barrie
J. Macdonald Oxley
J. S. Fletcher
J. S. Knowles
J. Storer Clouston
Jack London
Jacob Abbott
James Allen
James Andrews
James Baldwin
James Branch Cabell
James DeMille
James Joyce
James Lane Allen
James Lane Allen
James Oliver Curwood
James Oppenheim
James Otis
James R. Driscoll
Jane Austen
Jane L. Stewart
Janet Aldridge
Jens Peter Jacobsen
Jerome K. Jerome
John Burroughs
John Cournos
John F. Kennedy
John Gay
John Glasworthy

John Habberton
John Joy Bell
John Kendrick Bangs
John Milton
John Philip Sousa
Jonas Lauritz Idemil Lie
Jonathan Swift
Joseph A. Altsheler
Joseph Carey
Joseph Conrad
Joseph E. Badger Jr
Joseph Hergesheimer
Joseph Jacobs
Jules Vernes
Julian Hawthrone
Julie A Lippmann
Justin Huntly McCarthy
Kakuzo Okakura
Kenneth Grahame
Kenneth McGaffey
Kate Langley Bosher
Kate Langley Bosher
Katherine Cecil Thurston
Katherine Stokes
L. A. Abbot
L. T. Meade
L. Frank Baum
Latta Griswold
Laura Dent Crane
Laura Lee Hope
Laurence Housman
Lawrence Beasley
Leo Tolstoy
Leonid Andreyev
Lewis Carroll
Lewis Sperry Chafer
Lilian Bell
Lloyd Osbourne
Louis Hughes
Louis Tracy
Louisa May Alcott
Lucy Fitch Perkins
Lucy Maud Montgomery
Luther Benson
Lydia Miller Middleton
Lyndon Orr
M. Corvus
M. H. Adams
Margaret E. Sangster
Margret Howth
Margaret Vandercook

Margret Penrose
Maria Edgeworth
Maria Thompson Daviess
Mariano Azuela
Marion Polk Angellotti
Mark Overton
Mark Twain
Mary Austin
Mary Catherine Crowley
Mary Cole
Mary Hastings Bradley
Mary Roberts Rinehart
Mary Rowlandson
M. Wollstonecraft Shelley
Maud Lindsay
Max Beerbohm
Myra Kelly
Nathaniel Hawthrone
Nicolo Machiavelli
O. F. Walton
Oscar Wilde
Owen Johnson
P.G. Wodehouse
Paul and Mabel Thorne
Paul G. Tomlinson
Paul Severing
Percy Brebner
Peter B. Kyne
Plato
R. Derby Holmes
R. L. Stevenson
R. S. Ball
Rabindranath Tagore
Rahul Alvares
Ralph Bonehill
Ralph Henry Barbour
Ralph Victor
Ralph Waldo Emmerson
Rene Descartes
Rex Beach

Rex E. Beach
Richard Harding Davis
Richard Jefferies
Richard Le Gallienne
Robert Barr
Robert Frost
Robert Gordon Anderson
Robert L. Drake
Robert Lansing
Robert Lynd
Robert Michael Ballantyne
Robert W. Chambers
Rosa Nouchette Carey
Rudyard Kipling
Samuel B. Allison
Samuel Hopkins Adams
Sarah Bernhardt
Sarah C. Hallowell
Selma Lagerlof
Sherwood Anderson
Sigmund Freud
Standish O'Grady
Stanley Weyman
Stella Benson
Stella M. Francis
Stephen Crane
Stewart Edward White
Stijn Streuvels
Swami Abhedananda
Swami Parmananda
T. S. Ackland
T. S. Arthur
The Princess Der Ling
Thomas A. Janvier
Thomas A Kempis
Thomas Anderton
Thomas Bailey Aldrich
Thomas Bulfinch
Thomas De Quincey
Thomas Dixon

Thomas H. Huxley
Thomas Hardy
Thomas More
Thornton W. Burgess
U. S. Grant
Valentine Williams
Various Authors
Vaughan Kester
Victor Appleton
Victoria Cross
Virginia Woolf
Wadsworth Camp
Walter Camp
Walter Scott
Washington Irving
Wilbur Lawton
Wilkie Collins
Willa Cather
Willard F. Baker
William Dean Howells
William le Queux
W. Makepeace Thackeray
William W. Walter
William Shakespeare
Winston Churchill
Yei Theodora Ozaki
Yogi Ramacharaka
Young E. Allison
Zane Grey

www.ingramcontent.com/pod-product-compliance
Lightning Source LLC
Chambersburg PA
CBHW020503100426
42813CB00030B/3101/J